'This is the best history yet written of a British institution, alive to the cosmopolitan origins of food through global migration . . . a rewarding read for anyone interested in the history of Britain, so good in fact that it made me venture out on a windy night to buy a fish supper at my traditional local chippie.'
— *History Today*

'An affectionate, sprightly and crisply informative history of our national obsession.' — *Daily Mail*

'Full of fascinating facts.' — *The Spectator*

'What a clever, accessible, enjoyable, and informative book! While providing an abundance of revealing anecdotes, it also goes beyond food to tackle relevant topics such as migration, identity, technology, entrepreneurship, and more . . . a wonderful book.' — *Gastronomica*

'[A] scholarly account of the rise and enduring popularity of what Panayi presents as something of a cultural marvel.' — TLS

'*Fish and Chips* is a book brimming with fascinating facts and anecdotes about a dish that can be found on menus compiled by both Michelin Star chefs and your local chippy down the road.'
— *Oxford Times*

FISH AND CHIPS

A Takeaway History

Panikos Panayi

REAKTION BOOKS

Published by
Reaktion Books Ltd
Unit 32, Waterside
44–48 Wharf Road
London N1 7UX,
www.reaktionbooks.co.uk

First published 2014
Copyright © Panikos Panayi 2014
First published in paperback 2022

Printed and bound in Great Britain
by TJ Books Ltd, Padstow, Cornwall

A catalogue record for this book is available from the British Library

ISBN 978 1 78914 603 5

Contents

Preface

The roots of this book lie deep in my personal history. According to my parents fish and chips became one of the first solid foods I ate when we lived in Essex Road, Islington, in the early 1960s. While I can't remember this, I have a variety of childhood food memories, including the fact that I ate fish and chips every Friday well into my late adolescence from the same shop on Tottenham Lane (George's Fish Bar, still in existence) after we had moved to Hornsey in the middle of the 1960s. I did not question this rule for Friday-evening dining in our own house, which reflected countless others throughout Britain. If food consumption indicates integration, we had become true Britons, in my case almost from birth, despite the fact that I did not start speaking English until I went to school!

By the end of the 1970s, while remaining true to our Friday night takeaway habit, we started to diversify as other foods became increasingly available, whether Chinese, Indian, fried chicken or Wimpy. At the same time my younger sisters, Myllia and Rodothea, did not seem to have the same commitment to fish and chip eating as I and my parents had, although we did admittedly decide

Nestoras Iaonnou enjoying fish and chips at
Fisher's in Hunstanton, August 2012.

collectively to diversify. By the early 1980s fish and chips had lost its appeal for me.

While I did not leave home until 1989, I can't remember much fish and chip consumption during the 1980s or even the 1990s, when I lived in Stoke, Leicester and Osnabrück in Germany. I would eat a variety of takeaways, including the occasional fish and chips. In the last ten years, however, I have returned to my childhood love to the extent that I eat my favourite food once a week, although rarely on a Friday, whether from Oadby Fish Bar near my home in Leicester, the Cafe Fish Bar on North End Road, near Stamford Bridge, or Henry Higgins on the campus of De Montfort University. I also sample fish and chips either when making research trips in Britain or when I take holidays in the country with my wife, Mundeep. I certainly practise what I preach!

This book follows a tradition of volumes on fish and chips, of which I would like to single out five – three written by fryers, one by a journalist and another by a historian – spanning the period from the 1920s until the early 21st century. The list excludes handbooks, most notably Pierre Picton's *Gourmet's Guide to Fish and Chips*, originally published in 1966 and appearing in several editions since then.

The pioneering volume consisted of *The Fish Frier and His Trade*, written by William Loftas (aslo known as 'Chatchip') in the early 1920s, the first secretary of the National Federation of Fish Friers (the most important organization for preserving our dish and assisting those involved in it, and still highly active today, especially through the publication of the *Fish Friers Review*). In fact, *The Fish Frier and His Trade* consists of a collection of articles which Loftas had written for another magazine, the *Fish Trades Gazette*, under his pseudonym, providing details on the history of the trade and, more especially, information, as the subtitle suggests, on *How to Establish and Carry on an Up-to-date Fish Frying Business*. His book gave details on everything from the type of potatoes to use to the importance of the trade to the British economy.

In 1933 there followed the two-volume and 431-page *Modern Fish-frier* by H. T. Reeves, which takes a similar approach to Chatchip's book, focusing on how to set up a successful business and sell tasty food. Then, in 1968, the journalist Gerald Priestland published *Frying Tonight* at a time when Indian and Chinese take-aways appeared on the British high street as a new threat to the frying industry. Priestland's volume provided both a history of fish and chips and an analysis of the trade's contemporary situation, using his investigative journalistic skills, the *Fish Friers Review* and the *Fish Trades Gazette*.

The year 1992 saw the publication of the social historian John K. Walton's *Fish & Chips and the British Working Class, 1870–1940*. On the one hand, the range of dates might make this volume appear limited in its scope, but Walton's title suggests the link between our dish and the social group most closely associated with it. Walton, following Chatchip, also focuses upon the importance of the trade to the early twentieth-century British economy, as well as devoting much attention to the fish fryers themselves. The book represents an outstanding piece of social history. Numerous reviews greeted its appearance. The *Fish Friers Review* warmly welcomed it in its issue of March 1992. The reception in the broadsheets, on the other hand, resembled some of the condescending comments which had followed the dish itself throughout its history. David Buckley in the *Observer* of 1 March 1992 concluded that: 'John K. Walton's intriguing social observations are too buried beneath laborious scholarship to be easily digestible, but he does make you want to get some fish and chips.' In *The Guardian* of 29 February 1992 Martin Wainwright concentrated on an assertion in the book that fish and chips helped Britain to win the First World War because of its availability as cheap food for the working classes. The most sneering review came from Ben Macintyre in *The Times* of 4 April 1992 under the title of 'The Triumph of the Footnote', which ended: 'Dr Walton's conclusions may be reduced to a single, rather unsurprising fact: British working people like their fish and chips.'

The only significant book to appear since Walton's is Mark Petrou's *Fish and Chips*, published in 2010. Petrou, the son of a Greek Cypriot immigrant fryer and owner of a shop (Petrou Brothers) in Chatteris in Cambridgeshire, won the title of Fish and Chip Shop of the year in 2007. His book consists partly of autobiography, partly of potted history and partly of information on the current state of the trade.

As a professional historian, my own book most closely resembles Walton's, especially in terms of the methodology I have used, particularly the reading of publications issued by the trade, which provide vast amounts of information, especially the *Fish Friers Review* and the *Fish Trades Gazette*, together with numerous other books, magazines and articles on fish and chips. I have a different chronology from Walton, which covers the entire history of the trade since the middle of the nineteenth century to the present day. The book divides into five chapters covering 'Origins', 'Evolution', 'Britishness' and 'Ethnicity', allowing it to offer an insight into both the history and identity of fish and chips, tracing both the foreign elements of the dish and the way in which it became constructed as a national symbol. The final chapter on 'The Meanings of Fish and Chips' examines its significance in British life.

ONE

Origins

An official version of the origins of fish and chips, sanctioned by both the National Federation of Fish Friers (NFFF) and the Minister of Agriculture, Fisheries and Food, had become formalized in 1968, although it had problems from its outset. The NFFF had already begun celebrating 'the centenary of the marriage of fish and chips' in 1965 but also launched a search for the oldest establishment selling the dish in that year. The official ceremony, which took place in the Charing Cross Hotel on 26 September 1968, involved the Minister of Agriculture, Fisheries and Food, Cledwyn Jones, presenting a plaque to Denis Malin, recognized by the NFFF as the owner of the oldest fish and chip shop in the country, located at 560 Old Ford Road in the East End of London. The plaque described Malin's shop, established by Joseph Malin in 1860 and passed on to the current owner, Denis Malin, by his uncle Ernest Malin, as 'The World's Oldest Fish and Chip Business'. The NFFF had come to this conclusion after contacting its 120 regional associations in 1965

Cledwyn Jones, the Minister of Agriculture, Fisheries and Food (right), presenting a plaque to Denis Malin (left) at the Charing Cross Hotel on 26 September 1968, as recognized by the NFFF as the owner of the oldest fish and chip shop in the country, located at 560 Old Ford Road in the East End of London.

'asking them to submit any claims' they may have had about the world's oldest fish and chip shop. The choice came down to two: Malin's, and Lees's Chipped Potato Restaurant in Mossley, Lancashire, which does not appear to have sold fish at the time, as recognized by the NFFF when it launched its search in 1965. Nevertheless, a 'rebel from Lancashire . . . protested noisily throughout' the meeting at the Charing Cross Hotel in support of the claim of Lees.[1] More recently a plaque has gone up in Tommyfield Market in Oldham, the original site of an even earlier chip shop, claiming itself as the site of 'the first British fried chip' around 1860, 'from which the origins of Fish and Chip shops and the "Fast Food" industries can be traced'.[2]

While the fish and chip shop trade may have developed from the 1860s in the North, most evidence suggests that its origins lay in London. But if we accept this assertion, we again find ourselves faced with a semi-official version of the origins of fish and chips involving Henry Mayhew and Charles Dickens and focusing upon earlier decades of the nineteenth century. Thus an article in the *Daily Express* from 2010 begins: 'Generally it is accepted that this first fish and chip shop was opened by Joseph Malin in 1860' but also claims that 'chips had become a staple food of the industrial North of England while fried fish had been introduced to London's East End much earlier in the century', quoting an extract from *Oliver Twist* about a 'fried fish warehouse'.[3] Matthew Dennison in the *Daily Mail* used the same extract from Dickens, also in 2010.[4] This reference also appeared in *The Times* on 7 September 1957 and in the *Fish Friers Review* (FFR) of August 1949. Some popular books on fish and chips also use this evidence.[5] These references to Dickens, as well as to Henry Mayhew, go back to the first history of fish and chips, written in the form of an article by William Loftas, who went by the pseudonym 'Chatchip', the 'well-informed Manchester frier . . . who became the pioneer fish and chip trade journalist' by the 1920s, publishing regularly in the *Fish Trades Gazette* and bringing together his most important articles in *The Fish Frier and His Trade*, based upon 35 pieces which he wrote for the *Fish Trades Gazette* (FTG) running under the same title during 1921.[6] The second article in the series was entitled 'A Short History of the Fried-Fish Trade' with a section on 'The First Written Account of the Trade',

FISH AND CHIPS

quoting both *Oliver Twist* and, at much greater length, Henry Mayhew, the investigative journalist who published a series of sketches in the *Morning Chronicle* in 1849 and 1850 outlining life upon the streets of London. Mayhew actually identified sellers of fried fish, as did other contemporary sources, which concentrated particularly upon the Jewishness of these purveyors.[7]

The Early History of Fish and Potato Eating in Britain

There seems to be no evidence or reason to doubt the 'official' version of the origins of the fish and chip trade. The dish began to take off in the second half of the nineteenth century due to a series of economic and technological developments. Before examining these, however, we can briefly outline the longer-term history of potato and fish eating, especially in the British Isles. While some evidence suggests that the latter has Jewish origins (according especially to written accounts dated from throughout the nineteenth century, which stressed, in particular, eating fish that has been fried), cookery books published in London from the sixteenth, seventeenth and eighteenth centuries contain recipes for fish, whether fried or not. Potatoes also reached Britain during the early modern period but they did not become a staple part of the British diet, as in the case of fish, until the nineteenth century.

Fish consumption appears to have a history as old as humanity, although until the arrival of railways and refrigeration in the nineteenth century, which made preservation possible, only those living in coastal areas or near rivers could regularly eat fresh fish. Nevertheless from classical times methods of preserving fish evolved; salt usually played a central role, although the Greeks and the Romans both used a method of preserving tuna and mackerel which involved 'frying in oil, treating with bay leaves, salt, and spices and then pouring boiling vinegar over it'.[8] By Roman times fish farming also seems to have developed, while, for Jews and Christians, the consumption of fish had religious connotations.[9]

Fish consumption in Britain had taken off before the arrival of the Romans in the first century AD. Those people already present ate a wide variety of foods from the sea ranging from crabs to haddock, with preservation methods including wind drying and smoking.[10] The Roman invasion resulted in an increase in fish consumption, especially as the newcomers brought with them new methods of catching their prey. In London the eating of both sea and river fish became widespread.[11]

The departure of the Romans by the fifth century meant that some of the richer recipes for fish consumption went with them as a more ascetic Christianity became established. Eel farming, in which monasteries played an important role, became especially popular in the early medieval period. Inland fishing seems to have become widespread, particularly in areas with a ready supply of water, such as the Fens. By the time of the Norman invasion the use of nets had become common, meaning that herring fishing at sea had developed. Salt continued to play an important role in preservation. The first fishmongers appear to have evolved in the twelfth century – their guild dating back to 1154 – and at this stage they were catching as well as selling their wares.

Nevertheless most people in both Britain and Europe did not eat fish because of the problems of preservation. The most common method consisted of air drying. Herring, though, underwent a process of soaking in brine for about fifteen hours followed by barrelling between layers of salt; from the thirteenth century a method for smoking it evolved, although it would still need placing in barrels. And while even shellfish consumption also became common at this time, only the aristocracy tended to eat fresh fish. Cooking methods included spit-roasting, grilling on a gridiron, frying in oil, baking, stewing and poaching, encompassing most methods used today.[12]

The discovery of the New World had a significant impact upon fish consumption as a result of the arrival of a ready supply of cheap cod from the North Atlantic. Although French and Spanish fishermen had initially exploited the new supplies, the English became heavily involved over the course of the sixteenth and early seventeenth centuries so that ports in southwest England, including Plymouth, grew as fishing posts for North Atlantic cod fishing. Obviously the fish caught at this time had to undergo a drying process in which salt played an important role.[13]

'Fyshynge wyth an
Angle', woodcut.

The consumption of fish on Friday played an important role in
sustaining demand in Europe and Britain and would become so
ingrained in eating patterns that it would remain influential into the
twentieth century. The origins of this practice may lie in Judaic
traditions, but a series of other influences also helped to formalize it.
The Roman Catholic Church created days of abstinence from meat,
especially during holidays and Lent. Fish, however, remained an
exception from such rules for a variety of reasons.[14] According to
Mark Kurlansky, 'The medieval church imposed fast days on which
sexual intercourse and the eating of flesh were forbidden, but eating
"cold" foods was permitted. Because fish came from water, it was
deemed cold, as were waterfowl and whale, but meat was considered
hot food.'[15] This practice survived into post-Reformation England.
Attempts to enforce the observance of 'fysshe days' in the second half
of the sixteenth century 'must be attributed to the dearth of meat and

the needs of the navy that was to oppose Philip of Spain rather than to religious fervour'. Legislation actually came into operation imposing three meatless days per week, legislation which operated both during the sixteenth century and after the Restoration of the monarchy in the 1660s. While Britain may have become self-sufficient in food by the end of the seventeenth century, the practice of eating fish on a Friday would survive into the era of fish and chip eating from the end of the nineteenth century.[16]

Although cod became increasingly available during the early modern period, other types of fish also remained important, including herring and shellfish. Even so, by the eighteenth century improved methods of transportation meant that fresh fish became more visible in spite of the poor roads. For example, by 1724 tench, pike, perch and eels went from the Fens to London in fresh water barrels, with the water changed in the evening.[17] By the end of the eighteenth century ice came into use for the transportation of fresh salmon from Scotland to London.[18] Fishing techniques improved, including the use of longer fishing lines, allowing the capture of greater quantities of fish as well as the evolution of boats which could store their catches alive until they got to port.[19] Meanwhile, by the end of the eighteenth century the development of new methods of business enterprise helped the growth and supply of sea fish, partly fuelled by increasing population. Despite these innovations, salted, dried and pickled fish remained the most ready supply.[20]

By the seventeenth and eighteenth centuries fish had therefore become widely available in Britain and Europe, albeit overwhelmingly in preserved form. Most English cookbooks of this era carry a variety of recipes. We need to be slightly wary of their typicality because most refer to ways of cooking fresh rather than preserved fish, especially salmon, carp and pike, as well as seawater fish such as mullet, bream, herring, cod and shellfish.

Robert May's *The Accomplisht Cook* from 1671 provides a variety of recipes for a range of fish. Those for carp include two which involve boiling. The volume also suggests five ways of cooking pike: roasting, broiling, two methods of frying and how 'to make white Jelly of two Pikes'. The seven recipes for salmon include stewing, frying, boiling, broiling and roasting. Dressing 'Salmon in Stoffado' involves wine and a range of spices from rosemary to ginger and butter. May's book also contains a similar range of ways of cooking sturgeon and mullet.[21]

Interestingly many of these early modern cookbooks suggest the frying of fish, which, for those who could obtain it fresh, remained a common way of cooking it. *The Compleat Cook* from 1694 indicates ways of frying conger, lobsters, mullets, pike, salmon, sturgeon, turbot and halibut. One of the distinguishing features of these recipes consists of frying in butter, which inevitably meant shallow frying. Smaller fish cooked whole in this way, such as mullet, needed to be 'flowred', whereas larger specimens, such as sturgeon, needed cutting into pieces and cooking without flour. Spices and wine characterized some of these recipes such as that for 'turburt and holyburt' as well as pike.[22] Similarly T. Hall's *The Queen's Royal Cookery* from 1709 provided the following recipe for fried mullets:

> Scale, draw, and scotch them, wash them clean, wipe them dry, and flour them, fry them in clarified Butter, and being fryed, put them in a dish, put to them some Claret-wine, slic'd ginger, grated Nutmeg, a Anchovy, Salt and some sweet Butter, beat up thick, give the fish a walm with a minced Limon, and dish it, but first rub the Dish with a Clove of Garlick.[23]

A recipe for fresh cod from 1730 suggests the cooking of either cod, salmon, pike or carp in corbullion.[24]

At this stage in the history of fish consumption in Britain no clues exist that a revolution in fish frying would take place in the following century. Nevertheless, we find a recipe in perhaps the most famous English cookery book of the eighteenth century, by Hannah Glasse, in an edition from 1781, described as 'The Jews way of preserving Salmon and all sorts of fish'. This ran as follows:

> Take either salmon, cod, or any large fish, cut off the head, wash it clean, and cut it in slices as crimp'd cod is, dry it very

well in a cloth; then flour it, and dip it in yolks of eggs, and fry it in a great deal of oil, till it is of a fine brown, and well done; take it out and lay it to drain, till it is very dry and cold.

It seems somewhat presumptuous to suggest that here lie the origins of battered fish, not only because the batter seems completely different from that used from the early nineteenth century but because it seems more like a way of preserving the fish, as the title of the recipe suggests. In fact, if we read beyond the first few lines, Glasse then suggests placing the finished product in a jar filled with oil, vinegar and spices, which will 'keep good a twelvemonth'.[25]

By the early nineteenth century the method of frying fish suggested by Glasse appears to have become more widespread and closer to the method which would evolve in the fish and chip trade. M. Radcliffe's *Modern System of Domestic Cookery* (1823), in a section entitled 'Observations on Dressing Fish', provides the following instructions:

When fish is to be fried or broiled, it must be wrapped in a nice soft cloth after it is well cleansed and washed. When perfectly dry, wet with an egg, if for frying, and sprinkle the finest crumbs of bread over it; if done a second time with the egg and bread, the fish will look much better: then having a thick-bottomed frying-pan on the fire, with a large quantity of lard or dripping boiling hot, plunge the fish into it, and let it fry middlingly quick, till the colour is of a fine brown yellow and it is judged ready.

The recipe concluded that the fish 'should look a beautiful colour, and all the crumbs appear distinct'.[26] While this also does not quite appear to be the same as the battered fish which would become prevalent later in the century, it seems much closer to it than Glasse's recipe.

The course of the nineteenth century resulted in a mass increase in the supply of fresh fish. This would fuel the development of the fried fish trade, which took up a significant proportion of the catch. While population growth acted as an underlying driving force,

Victorian Billingsgate, 1876, etching.

technological developments came together to bring fresh fish to the masses. Even as late as 1850 'most of the fish consumed in Britain was either dried, salted or smoked, in various combinations', so that only the wealthy could still afford fresh fish either caught close to the coast or in rivers. The consumption of freshwater fish actually declined as fresh sea fish, even from distant waters, became increasingly prevalent.[27]

'It was the railway, followed by the use of ice and steam trawling, that revolutionised the habits of fish consumption in this country, and converted fish from something in the nature of an expensive luxury food into a food of the working classes.'[28] In 1813 a committee which examined the fish supply of London anticipated developments which would occur over the following decades and suggested a series of methods of transporting the produce of the sea to the capital more quickly, including the construction of a 'railway'.[29] By 1856 fish caught off the Norfolk coast and taken to Yarmouth and Lowestoft would leave the coast every evening and reach Billingsgate – which had undergone significant expansion and renovation in the 1850s – the next morning. Similarly, by this time fish came by railway to

Billingsgate from Scotland, as well as from south coast ports and Devon and Cornwall.[30] As George Dodd's account of London's food supply pointed out in 1856, rail 'almost annihilates distance'. In Billingsgate:

> There is salmon from the Tweed, the Tay, the Forth, the Clyde, the Dee, the Don, the Spey, the Ness, the Linn; there is cod from Holland, from Norway, from the Yarmouth coast; there are brill, turbot, halibut, sole, plaice, haddock, whiting, and skate, all trawl-fish (caught by trawl-net), and brought from nearly the same waters as the cod; there are mackerel from Devon and Cornwall, eels from Holland, oysters from the Thames and the Channel Islands, lobsters from the coasts of Scotland and Norway, crabs from the south coast, shrimps from the Thames and Boston.[31]

Such a scene would have been inconceivable even 30 years earlier. By this time 932,340,000 wet fish (263,381,000 lbs/119,467,600 kg) were sold 'in the streets of London'.[32]

The railway therefore completely transformed fish consumption in London; the rest of the country followed as large northern cities developed significant fish markets in the second half of the nineteenth

A serving of fish and chips, 2012.

century. While Liverpool had three fishmongers in 1843, the number had increased to 50 within twenty years.[33] The growing use of ice in the first half of the nineteenth century also had a major role to play in fish supply. It came from a variety of sources: for example, farmers in the 'Thames marshes' gathered it from ditches and canals. At the same time, importation occurred from Norway and even the USA. Each port constructed its own ice house. Only in the 1890s, however, did the production of artificial ice become a mainstay, allowing fishing to take place even further away from a home port.[34] By this time large-scale trawlers had also become prominent. Trawling had begun to gain importance from the seventeenth century; it would undergo significant growth as the nineteenth century progressed, particularly as steamships took over from sail, which, together with the artificial creation of ice, allowed ships to travel further afield and preserve fresh fish.[35] These developments meant that the scene described by George Dodd at Billingsgate in 1856 spread to the rest of the country as one of the raw materials for fish and chips had become commonplace by the second half of the nineteenth century.

However, our story has two elements to it and before discussing the marriage of fish and chips in the second half of the nineteenth century, we need to outline the history of the potato, especially in Britain. Like many other products which became staples in Europe and elsewhere after the discovery of the New World, the potato has its origins in the Western Hemisphere and, more particularly, in South America. More precisely potatoes came from the Andes, especially Peru, Chile and Bolivia, with a history dating back over 8,000 years. Spanish adventurers first came across them in the 1530s and they appear to have reached Spain by the 1580s at the very latest and perhaps even as early as 1560. By 1600 they had also arrived in Italy, Austria, Belgium, Holland, France, Switzerland, England, Germany and probably Ireland and Portugal. At this stage, however, they only interested botanists and did not take off as a food product because many European peasantries viewed them with suspicion and even fear.[36] Their arrival in England during the 1580s appears to be linked with Sir Walter Raleigh and his companion Thomas Herriott, although some dispute appears to exist over the precise details of how they made their way to the country.[37]

Acceptance of the potato as a staple food in Europe remained a slow process and it appears that the first people to have adopted it were the Irish. This can be explained by the fact that 'it suited the soil, climate, and living conditions remarkably well', but also by the fact that for the peasantry, it acted 'as a safeguard, however meagre, against the tandem social plagues of unemployment, poverty, overpopulation, and land hunger', which, by 1780, 'had helped push the tuber to dominance'. By the beginning of the nineteenth century many Irish people consumed 5½ lbs (2.5 kg) of potatoes per day, almost always boiled, although some frying also took place, as did mashing and mixing with other root vegetables to create colcannon.[38]

In England the potato took longer to become universally accepted and during the seventeenth century it appears to have remained a luxury crop. It first took off in Lancashire at the end of the seventeenth century, perhaps because of the proximity of Ireland.[39] According to the most authoritative history of the potato a more important factor lay in the fact that oat production dominated over wheat here. Salaman suggests that potatoes could make more progress in areas of predominantly oat cultivation because those who ate the poor quality bread it produced were more willing to eat potatoes.[40]

The potato made inroads into the diet of the lower classes during the late eighteenth century and would make a significant breakthrough during the course of the early nineteenth due to some of the fundamental changes in English economy and society of this period. For much of the eighteenth century the population of England, especially those who lived in areas where wheat predominated, appear to have enjoyed a healthy diet which included vegetables, fruit and dairy products but lacked meat. A combination of population growth, industrialization and movement to towns would change this situation. From the 1790s in particular, partly because of a series of bad harvests which lasted from this decade until the end of the Napoleonic Wars in 1815, potatoes began to gain a foothold, which would gradually strengthen during the course of the early nineteenth century as they increasingly became a staple of the working-class diet. As wheat cultivation declined potato cultivation grew. From 1770 until 1840, as bread became more expensive, the cultivation of potatoes increased while their price decreased. The fact that people moved to inner-city accommodation, and the attendant difficulty of baking bread daily as had been done in the countryside, also helped the decline in the traditional loaf, primarily because of lack of access to ovens. Urban allotments developed in which potatoes became the main crop. Furthermore, industrialization resulted in a fall in real terms of the wages of the labouring classes, a development exacerbated from the second half of the eighteenth century by the growth in population. At no time, however, did the potato come to play the dominant role in England which it would do in Ireland, leading to the catastrophe of the famine in the middle of the 1840s.[41]

The second of our main staples for fish and chips had become the food of the people by the time this dish took off in the second half of the nineteenth century. But relatively few references exist to the consumption of fried potatoes in Britain until this period. *The Accomplisht Cook* from 1671 does actually use the term 'Italian Chips' but the recipe that follows involves 'some paste of flowers' beaten 'to fine powder', 'gum dragon steeped in rose-water' beaten 'to a perfect paste in a marble morter', then rolled thinly and combined together 'so that they will look of divers pretty colours like marble'.[42] The only link with nineteenth-century chips perhaps consists of the shape.

Cooking of potatoes in England, however, did not generally involve frying before the nineteenth century, although it did occur. Potatoes took a long time to become a side dish, still regarded as exotic until the early nineteenth century. One eighteenth-century cookbook indicates that the most common way of cooking consisted of boiling, which resulted in consumption with various types of 'sauces' such as gravy, 'ketchup', salt and pepper or spices. Recipes also existed for eating them with herrings or meat by this period.[43] A century earlier some recipes suggested using sweetener with potatoes and this tradition survived until the end of the eighteenth century. By the early nineteenth people in Cornwall consumed corned fish with potatoes. Some Devonians may also have eaten fried fish and chipped potatoes at this time.[44] A reference from the *Fish Friers Review* of January 1959 provided by C. J. Robb of Ballyminch, Co. Down, entitled 'Fish and Chips 200 Years Ago' claimed to have found a letter written in 1760 by 'Dolly Brown, the celebrated Irish beauty at the Court in Dublin' in which she often ate 'fried fish with potato fingers, cooked till brown'. Radcliffe's *Modern System of Domestic Cookery* suggests several ways of cooking potatoes including boiling and roasting. He also includes three ways of frying: cold potatoes fried in dripping; potatoes fried whole; and 'Potatoes Fried in Slices or Shavings' as follows:

> Peel large potatoes, slice them about a quarter of an inch thick, or cut them in shavings round and round as you would peel a lemon; dry them well in a clean cloth, and fry them in lard or dripping. Take care that your fat and frying pan are quite clean; put it on a quick fire, watch it, and as soon as the lard boils, and is still, put in the slices of potatoes, and keep moving them till they are crisp; take them and lay them to drain on a sieve; serve them up with a very little salt sprinkled over them.[45]

Fried potato consumption in Britain takes off at about the same time as it develops in France, suggesting either some sort of culinary transfer from one country to the other, or the development of potato frying in both countries simultaneously. In both cases the frying of this vegetable developed when its consumption increased so that this method of cooking would have offered a more flavoursome alternative to boiling. The method of cooking, rather than the shape of the chopped or chipped potato, is what matters.[46]

The Marriage of Fish and Chips

While the marriage of fish and chips appears to have happened at some stage during the middle of the nineteenth century, the two products came separately to prominence as street foods in the earlier part of the century. Here we can return to the two classic sources quoted in the standard histories of our dish in the form of Dickens and Mayhew. The main reference quoted from Dickens actually comes from *Oliver Twist*, originally published in 1838. The extract does not tell us very much, simply mentioning the presence of a 'fried-fish warehouse' in a 'dismal alley leading to Saffron Hill' where 'Snow Hill and Holborn Hill' meet.[47] Interestingly, Dickens speaks of a warehouse rather than a shop, suggesting that it acted as the headquarters for other fried fish dealers. Yet how could preservation of the product which would come to prominence later in the century take place in a warehouse? Such fish must have had more in common with the type described by Hannah Glasse than it did with the fresh, hot, battered type. The other reference in Dickens comes from *A Tale of Two Cities*, the historical novel set in Paris and London before and during the French Revolution in the 1780s and '90s. This makes a reference to 'husky chips of potato, fried with some reluctant drops of oil' available in the Saint-Antoine suburb of Paris.[48] According to the editor of the Oxford edition of the novel of 1998, Andrew Sanders, 'this would appear the first modern use of the word "chips" applied to fried pieces of potato'.[49]

Sanders also points us to Henry Mayhew who provides much information on fried fish in London in this era, as well as a few details about potato consumption. Mayhew spent much time describing the sellers of 'wet-fish, dry-fresh and shell-fish', which had now become cheap food as a result of its increasing availability. The 'agency of the costermongers . . . conveyed' this 'cheap food' to 'every poor man's door'.[50] Londoners could also purchase cooked and prepared fish including 'pea soup and hot eels' and 'pickled whelks'.[51] Mayhew also counted between 250 and 350 purveyors of fried fish and claimed that this product had become available over 'many years'. The sellers 'are for the most part, old men and boys' as well 30 or 40 women and three or four girls. The main type of fish consisted of sole and plaice 'dabs', a 'common word for any flat fish', with plaice providing 'upwards of one half the quantity' of fried fish available; 'the other fishes used are soles, haddocks, whitings, flounders, and herrings, but very sparingly indeed as regards herrings'. The fish

A baked potato
seller in Victorian
London, 1861,
etching.

came from Billingsgate. Some consisted 'of the overplus of a fishmonger's stock, of what he has not sold overnight and does not care to offer for sale on the following morning, and therefore vends it to the costermongers, whose customers are chiefly among the poor'. Mayhew described the preparation of the fish for sale:

> The fish to be fried is first washed and gutted; the fins, head, and tail are then cut off, and the trunk is dipped in flour and water, so that in frying, oil being always used, the skin will not be scorched by the, perhaps, too violent action of the fire, but merely browned. Pale rape oil is generally used.

Jews in Victorian London, print.

The cooking took place 'in ordinary frying pans'. Mayhew claimed that fish fryers lived in poor accommodation throughout London, where their practice led to complaints from their neighbours because of the smell. Most consisted of itinerant sellers, while some used stationary stalls. The former usually went from one public house to another 'in populous neighbourhoods', while others sold their produce at 'races and fairs' to stable boys in particular. At public houses the fish often came with a slice of bread. One seller in his forties interviewed by Mayhew had worked for seventeen years in the trade, after initially selling oysters, which had become dangerous because of the number of times he had cut his hands opening them.[52] Mayhew makes no mention of fried potatoes but does have information on itinerant baked potato sellers, who, however, remain separate from those purveying fried fish.[53]

Mayhew therefore provides much information on fried fish but no clue on chips. A series of newspaper articles and other publications from mid-nineteenth century London confirm Mayhew's findings without providing the same level of detail. Many of these simply link fried fish with the poor or the Jews and those who wrote of the latter often used anti-Semitic stereotypes.[54] Even those articles that do not dwell on these issues often point to the social status or ethnicity of the purveyors.

The earliest reference to an itinerant fried fish seller comes from an article in the *Morning Chronicle* of 7 April 1824, which mentions, in a piece on a boxing match, Aby Belasco, who 'was occupied in frying fish and cooking other victuals for refreshment on the road'. Thirteen years later this newspaper carries a report, also available in other publications, about a 'Frightful Death by Burning'. This involved 'Mrs Rebecca Mendes, a Jewess, 47 years of age', who lived in Church Lane in Whitechapel and 'obtained a living by frying and hawking fried fish'. Her death actually happened because the pan which she used caught fire.[55] A report on a court case from 1840 in which the plaintiff 'was a hook nosed Jew, named Abrahams' pointed out, confirming one of Mayhew's findings, that 'The Jew was a dealer in fried fish, with which he visited the public houses in the neighbourhood.'[56] Another newspaper article from 1840 supports Mayhew's assertion of fried fish being sold 'in many of the divisions of London'.[57] Two years later another newspaper article mentions Jeremy East, 'a vendor of those delightful delicacies which are to be seen in the neighbourhood of the galleries of our minor theatres, and known to the populace by the name of "fried dab"'. The report actually referred to a court case in Bow Street involving two youths who had stolen a fried fish from East.[58] In 1851 we learn of a case against a Mr Robinson who used his premises in Queen's Terrace in Chelsea 'for frying fish in dripping . . . The fish was cut up and sold to people of the humbler classes in the neighbourhood.'[59] One of the most interesting of these titbits of information comes from an article in the *Royal Cornwall Gazette* of 10 October 1851, which claims to quote *The Times*, although a search of various newspaper indexes, including that of *The Times*, does not confirm this. The piece concerned mentions that the 'swarms' of London often gravitate towards the river in the summer, including Battersea. 'Cold fried fish, pickled onions, pettitoes, and "hot pickled eels" are among the choicest comestible on sale.' Unfortunately the article provides little other information.

More usefully we have a description of a fried fish shop around the time of Mayhew, without quite the empathy which Mayhew provides. It comes from a book entitled *The Wild Tribes of London*, who include the Jews of Petticoat Lane. On a tour of the neighbourhood the author, Watts Phillips, comes across a 'most delectable odour' and a 'bubbling, fizzling sound' from a fish shop which 'throws its cheerful glare into the chilly night . . . one of many of a similar character which abound in the neighbourhood'. The author then provides an interesting description of events inside.

> The first thing which arrests our attention, after having feasted our eyes upon the rows of crisp brown fish that decorate the window, is the large fire within, which has a fiercely jolly look, like the face of a giant who has taken to drinking . . . The shop is tenanted by a family of five – a mother, her three daughters, and an only son . . . The mother . . . stands by the fire, the presiding genius of the frying-pan, whose handle she holds firmly, as hardy mariner the good ship's helm. She grasps her fork like a harpoon, and, with a steady eye, watches the sea of hissing, bubbling oil. Each moment the fork descends, and transfixes a fish, till one by one the rich brown spoil lies heaped up within the confines of the dish, while the frying-pan bubbles and hisses with impatience, calling loudly, like the horse-leech's daughter, for more . . .
>
> The elder daughter of the house stands near her mother . . . She is cutting the fish in slices, preparing them for their hot bath in the hissing pan; and we shiver as we hear the keen knife crash through the bone, and strike the table beneath.[60]

Despite the claims of the National Federation of Fish Friers, the early history of fish and chips remains a hazy one and, as several researchers have discovered, the marriage of fish and chips may not have taken place at a particular place in a particular moment, but did so gradually. For much of the second half of the nineteenth century, fish and potatoes had their own separate purveyors. Indeed, John Walton pointed out that fried fish dealers remained distinct from chip dealers until the 1890s in some parts of Lancashire. He also asserts that baked potatoes had become common in the Oldham area by the 1850s, which mirrors London and possibly other parts of the country.[61] Mark Petrou questions both the Lancashire and London versions of the origins of fish and chips.[62] Priestland, meanwhile, pointed to 'a gap between the years 1860 and 1880', which he tried to fill by investigating the history of Malin's shop, originally in Cleveland Street in Bethnal Green but also Lees's, which he confirmed sold chips but not fish.[63]

In the third quarter of the nineteenth century most evidence suggests that fried fish and potato selling remained separate and that it was not until the end of the century that fish and chip shops became common, partly as a result of the efforts of manufacturers of standardized equipment. A variety of sources, especially newspapers, point to the fact that, in the final decades of the nineteenth century, fried fish in particular had moved from London to the provinces.

Cookbooks and recipe columns point to the separate lives of fried fish and fried potatoes during the nineteenth century. Alexis Soyer's *A Shilling Cookery Book for the People* carries a recipe for 'fried potatoes', which involves cutting them 'into very thin slices, almost shavings', mirroring a similar recipe in a seminal Anglo-Jewish cookbook of the nineteenth century, which used the phrase 'potato shavings'.[64] Soyer also provides an alternative method with the name of 'Fried Cooked Potatoes', involving slightly thicker slices.[65] By the 1880s at the latest fried potatoes had come to resemble the shape of those found in fish and chip shops, as indicated in a recipe from the *Girl's Own Paper* of 31 July 1886:

> To return to our fried potatoes: the best for the purpose as giving the least trouble, are large and longish ones, as they should be cut lengthwise in finger-shaped pieces. We presume it is understood that they must be raw ones. After having been pared, washed, drained, and dried in a cloth, they are

put in the boiling fat, and if quite covered they require no moving about until they become of a golden colour, when they are taken out, put in a drainer for a few seconds, and lastly, sprinkled with salt before being served.

Earlier in the 1880s the same newspaper had provided a recipe for frying fish, which needed encasing 'in an outer covering, in order to preserve the juices. This may consist of flour . . . [it] may be formed also of a thick batter of flour and water, of frying batter, and of beaten egg and bread or water biscuit crumbs.'[66] This mirrors recipes dating back to Hannah Glasse, although the *Girl's Own Paper* does not deal with any issues of ethnicity or nationality, unlike Soyer, who gave a recipe involving dipping halibut in a batter of water and flour and then deep frying, which he described as 'Fried Fish, Jewish Fashion'.[67] By the time Soyer published his *Shilling Cookery Book*, recipe books purely about fish had emerged, reflecting the availability of fresh seafood by this time. One of the earliest of these, from 1854, contains a section on 'How to Fry Fish', which outlined a six-stage process involving preparing the pan, the oil and the fish. In stage five, 'the fish itself should be thoroughly dried and folded in a cloth, and either well dredged with flour, or completely coated with egg and bread crumb'.[68] In 1883 *Fish Cookery*, by Mrs John B. Thwaites, described fish frying as 'such an important branch of cookery'; she actually suggested three batters, depending upon the fish which needed frying.[69]

Such recipes entered cookbooks at the same time as ready-fried fish spread throughout the country and as fried potatoes began to make their presence felt in the streets competing alongside baked potatoes. Newspaper and magazine articles help to illustrate the spread of chips and fried fish. Such articles suggest that, rather than marrying, the two products courted and gradually moved in together as the century progressed.

References to fried fish in London surface fairly regularly, often linked with Jewish settlement. James Greenwood claimed that in 1867 'in nine cases out of ten the fish purchased' in 'Squalors Market' in London 'was intended for the frying-pan . . . This universal fish-frying is the key to another mystery common to the neighbour-hood' in the form of 'solid slabs of a tallowy-looking substance' found in numerous shops. This was dripping: 'Mutton suet and boiled rice are the chief ingredients used in the manufacture of the slabs, the gravy of bullocks' kidneys being stirred into the mess when it is half cold, giving to the whole a mottled and natural appearance.'[70] At about the same time as this we learn that the food of London dockers 'is cold saveloys, cold fried fish, cold bread and cheese . . . washed down with a dark, repulsive-looking fluid which is called beer'.[71] In 1872 an article in the *Morning Post* on 'Street Cookery' in London pointed out that: 'Fried fish are in greatest demand on Saturday evenings, when they are eagerly bought by workmen and their wives going to, or coming from, the market.' The practices recognized by Mayhew continued:

> In the eastern and southern districts the fried fish trade is pursued separately by men who have fixed rounds, who call at every public house on their beats, and who find a ready sale for the browned and crisp slices in bar parlours and tap rooms. Plaice and soles are the fish which are usually fried; but sometimes, when prices are low, whiting and cod, and even mackerel and herring find a place in the tray of the fish seller. Those who are engaged in this traffic invariably fry the fish themselves. The oil or dripping which they use is too frequently rancid, and the cookery is rarely good; but notwithstanding these shortcomings purchasers are numerous and the occupation is profitable.[72]

In 1879 an article in *Chambers's Journal* stated that 'you must go to the East End to taste fried fish in perfection'.[73] The number of fires caused in fried fish shops also suggests that their numbers had grown in the capital, increasing from eight in 1867 to eleven in 1888.[74]

By this time fried fish had spread beyond London. Several stories surface in the provincial press from the 1860s complaining about its smell. A letter to the editor of the *Manchester Courier* in 1866 asked whether local authorities could 'prohibit the sale of fried fish, which is becoming such a great nuisance to the inhabitants in the neighbour-hoods where it is sold'.[75] In Leicester and nearby Hinckley complaints emerged about fried fish in 1869.[76] An article in the *Birmingham Daily Post* of 19 June 1874, after expressing astonishment 'at the enormous quantities of fish' now available in 'our local Billingsgate', continued that the 'number of fried fish shops in almost every street . . . point to the article they purvey as an indispensable gastronomic commodity in the household economy of many of our population'.

The sale of potatoes also developed during the third quarter of the nineteenth century and beyond. The baked variety continued to thrive, sometimes combined with fried fish. The sellers of the former product identified by Mayhew continued to make a living into the 1870s.[77] As early as 1868 a customer called at a shop in Westgate Hill in Newcastle where he 'had fried-fish with baked potatoes and pick-les at the counter, and paid 6d. for the dish' although the owner, John Cager, faced a fine of £5 for selling fried fish without a licence.[78] At fairs in Humberstone Gate in Leicester in the 1870s 'various del-icacies in the way of mussels, pickles, potatoes, and fried fish, were well represented.'[79] Similarly, visitors to Hampstead Heath on Good Friday in 1884 found that 'hunger and thirst were provided for by tea and coffee stalls, fried fish and baked potato stalls, ice-barrows, &c.'[80] By this time fish and chip shops had certainly surfaced, although purveyors sometimes sold this delicacy without a licence under the Refreshment House Act and therefore faced fines. They included Charles Silverstone, whose business appears to have lain in the West End, and William Allen, who kept 'a small shop for the sale of fried fish and potatoes, at 103, Bethnal-green-road'.[81] By 1883 a 'slice of fried fish, fried potatoes, and a slice of bread can be had for threepence'. The 'fried-fish men clear the market at Billingsgate of anything that may be going cheap – plaice and skate'.[82]

The Spread of the Fish and Chip Trade

Whenever the actual marriage of fish and chips took place and wherever the first fish and chip shop may have surfaced, from the 1870s the working classes could buy cheap food in the form of fish and chips in the street, in public houses, at fairs or, increasingly, in shops built for this purpose so that thousands of such establishments existed by the outbreak of the First World War throughout the country. One estimate suggested that between 10,000 and 12,000 fried fish shops had emerged in Britain by 1888, a figure which had increased to 25,000 by 1910. By 1906 London alone may have counted as many as 1,200. By this time a 5-mile radius around Manchester Town Hall may have been home to 2,000 fried fish shops, while 500 may have existed in Oldham. They had also emerged in seaside resorts by the start of the twentieth century.[83]

Such statistics suggest a rapid spread of the fish and chip trade at the end of the nineteenth century. The reasons for this spread revolve around the increasing supply of fish and potatoes, helped by the technological developments described above. Fish and chips may have taken up 20 per cent of the fish caught by British trawlers on the eve of the First World War and perhaps 10 per cent of the potatoes grown in Britain.[84]

These supply-side factors found reception in the demand side in the form of the British working classes. Despite the constant sneering from educated commentators, which has greeted this dish since its inception in the middle of the nineteenth century, it offered a nutritious, cheap and tasty food for those at the lower end of the social scale in an era in which poverty and poor nutrition characterized many working lives indicated by the 'consistently high level of infant mortality' as late as the 1890s.[85] One article from 1885, entitled 'Fish and Potatoes: A Weakness', commented on the entire experience of eating this dish including witnessing 'the grace in the peculiar potato-cutting, guillotine-shaped instrument that one sees in nearly every fried-fish shop' and 'the pleasant hiss and splatter of the frying fat, and the savoury odour that comes on the snowy wings of steam from the open door, to salute the olfactory organs of the hungry

An early fish and chip shop, 1905.

passers-by'. The writer continued that: 'when one places his hard-earned twopence on the counter' he 'receives in exchange the hot, fragrant, nicely-browned piece of fish, and the potatoes done to a turn'.[86] This extract essentially deals with the issue of taste and the consequent attention to our dish from this point of view.

The arrival of fish and chips in the late nineteenth century would have had a similar culinary impact to the coming of Chinese and then 'Indian' food in the decades after the Second World War.[87] Like these two types of cuisine, we might see fish and chips as a fad, one of the first in the history of the takeaway in Britain, but one which has lasted a long time. Nonetheless, Olive Malvery, a journalist who had decided to experience 'the life of the poor and working classes', became convinced that fish and chip shops 'play a very important role in the social and domestic economy of London's poor. From these shops many a workman's wife is able to provide an ample meal for six or even eight mouths for as small a sum as 6d' while also saving on 'the expense and trouble of cooking' as fuel 'is a heavy item in small wages; therefore, cheap and good cooked food is certainly an advantage to the people'.[88] This would help to explain why, in some northern towns, there may have existed one fish and chip shop for every 1,000 inhabitants, in some cases falling to as low as one in 400.[89]

Business reasons also played a role in the development of the trade, supported by legislation. Despite complaints about the smell of fish frying (initially recognized by Mayhew), the Public Health Act of 1875, amended in 1891, 1896 and 1907, tried to deal with this issue by introducing controls on emissions.[90] The fish and chip trade also represented a relatively easy and cheap way of becoming self-employed, with many of those who set up a business emerging from the skilled working classes with little capital. The shops that opened towards the end of the nineteenth century evolved from Mayhew's earlier itinerant fish fryers, even though such travelling salesman would continue into the twentieth century. Adverts in the *FTG* from 13 October 1883 for shops in London suggest prices of £30 or £40 for premises. In many areas prices would remain cheap, although they increased in some big cities as fish and chips grew in popularity. Those who moved into the business could take out loans, while others inherited money. For example, Tom Baldwin obtained £10 when his uncle died in 1900. He had previously worked as a railway porter and a labourer in a potato warehouse. Initially purchasing a small business, he sold this with a significant profit, which also allowed him to move to a larger house.[91]

The availability of standardized equipment also allowed the fish and chip shop to develop because it provided a ready-made template which those who moved into the business could follow, a pattern which Indian restaurants would adapt from the 1960s and 1970s.[92] Faulkner and Co. may have manufactured ranges for frying chips from the early 1870s while John Rouse claimed to have developed a mobile range for frying fish and chips in the 1880s.[93] The earliest range suggested by Chatchip, with accompanying diagram, actually simply consisted of two removable bowls in brick casing, under which the fire burned. The first variation on this model involved adding a steam extractor.[94] By the beginning of the twentieth century potato peelers and chippers had also became available. Metal ranges

Sketch A.

A. Sketch showing the type of range first built for fish and chip frying. The bricks used were of the ordinary red type. There was no hot plate. The pans were built into the brickwork, and the top surface of the range was simply plastered over with a thick coat of mortar. The latter very frequently cracked with the heat, and the whole body of the range after a very short time became saturated with oil or fat. When hot the whole body of the range would reek with oil and fat fumes, which, added to the clouds of steam emanating from the open pans—when cooking was in process, and which there was no effort to control—created a stench which penetrated into the nostrils of passengers within a quarter of a mile radius.

Sketch B.

B. Sketch showing shape of frying-pans originally used. These pans were about 18 inches deep. They held gallons of oil, and took no end of coal to keep up to boiling pitch

The foregoing sketches were drawn from a range which until a few years ago could be seen in a shop in Salford. It was at the time I saw it said to have been there for over fifty years, and the accumulation of burnt congealed starch on the top surface was then in places some seven or eight inches thick.

In the better-class shops the brickwork was given a periodical coat of whitewash, but when, as often happened, the oil in the body of the range oozed through to the front surfaces there were some curious artistic (?) effects produced.

The earliest frying range from the later Victorian period.

such as Faulkner's 'Kensington', which would gradually come to prominence, had also emerged.[95]

Fish fryers had developed their own identity by the early twentieth century through the formation of their own organization. Although some early groupings had already emerged, the National Federation of Fish Friers came into existence in 1913 and survives into the present day. While suspicion may play a role in dealings between members, it has helped to spread expertise. Its emergence suggests similar experiences and identities existed before 1913.[96]

The Birth of Fish and Chips

Fish and chips emerged in Britain during the second half of the nineteenth century when fried fish combined with chipped potatoes. While the standardized history provided by the NFFF may prove tempting, it seems that fish and chips came together in a more haphazard way. There seems little doubt that Mayhew's fryers paved the way and the developments which would take place later in the century involved a sedentarization of the people he came across. They served customers with similarly low levels of disposable income but the fish and chip shop owners had added potatoes to their meal, unlike Mayhew's fryers, who gave their customers bread. As a series of newspaper reports indicate, the move from bread to chips took place gradually with a transitional phase in which baked potatoes sometimes accompanied fish. The availability of frying oil and dripping may have played a role in the spread of the chip, partly as a by-product of industrialization in the case of widely used cotton seed oil.[97]

A whole series of factors gave rise to the birth and early spread of our dish but the most important surely consisted of the availability of fresh fish, which transformed this food from that of the wealthy to that of the masses. The coming of the railways clearly played a key role as Mayhew and Dodd recognized. Developments later in the century, including the steam trawler and the increasing availability of ice, helped the spread of fresh fish beyond London. At the same time, a series of economic factors, especially in the early nineteenth century, enabled the potato to become an increasingly important

Old Keswickian, May 2012, run by the same extended family since the 1980s.

carbohydrate not simply in Ireland and parts of northern Britain, but in the whole country. The availability, cheapness and nutritional value of fresh fish and potatoes acted as the bedrock upon which the fish and chip industry would be built.

TWO

Evolution

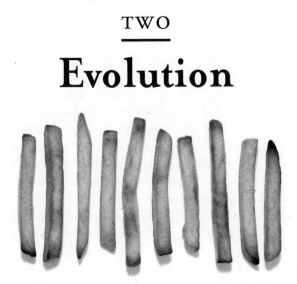

By the beginning of the twentieth century fish and chips had emerged from the itinerant fish fryers of Victorian London and the chip sellers of Lancashire to unite in the form in which it would become recognized and accepted. By the outbreak of the First World War as many as 25,000 fish and chip shops may have existed in Britain. By this time the purveyors of this meal had also established their own organization in the form of the NFFF.

We might view the history of fish and chips over the past 100 years as one of rise and decline. In this scenario it reigns supreme as the takeaway of choice for the working classes until the 1960s, after which it faces competition, initially from the newly arrived Italian and, more especially, Chinese and Indian takeaways and, more threateningly, from the big U.S. multinationals like Kentucky Fried Chicken and, above all, McDonalds. The arrival of these alternatives helped to confirm the stereotype of fish and chips as the food of the British working classes, in contrast to these new meals, superficially symbolic of a more multicultural and globalized Britain.

The zenith of fish and chips lasted from the First World War to the 1960s, by which time newspaper columnists had started to comment on the decline of the fish and chip shop, especially as a result of the threat of 'foreign' competition. Since that time the relative decline of the industry has taken place. However, while the number of businesses may have fallen, their total numbers remain as high as most takeaway competitors. The narrative which follows will examine the issue of zenith and decline by paying particular attention to the nature of the business and the food served.

Zenith

The decades between the First World War and the 1960s form the high point in the history of fish and chips in Britain. As we have seen, one estimate claimed that the number of shops in Britain had already reached 25,000 by 1910 and similar estimates circulated for decades to come. Unofficial and, increasingly, official figures help us to give a fairly accurate assessment of the trade for much of the earlier twentieth century. As we shall see, the industry took in a good

proportion of the white fish brought to Britain, as well as the potatoes grown in the country. When the supply of these declined, the
price of the dish increased, a pattern which would continue for much
of the century.

In 1921 Chatchip (aka William Loftas, the fish and chip
commentator) claimed that at least 25,000 fish and chip shops existed
in Britain and that they accounted for at least 25 per cent of the fish
consumed in the country. He also asserted that the trade directly
employed at least 75,000 people; a total which increased to 100,000
if one included those who serviced the shops such as equipment
manufacturers. It also found 'indirect employment for many
thousands more'. His statistics 'prove that at least 30,000,000 meals
per week are distributed through the fried fish shops of Great Britain'.[1]
By the middle of the 1920s and into the 1930s and beyond official
figures confirm some of these findings but also suggest some
exaggeration. In 1926 a report on the marketing of potatoes in Britain
'estimated that about 15 per cent of the potatoes consumed pass
through the hands of the "chip" trade. The effect is most noticeable
in some factory towns, especially in South Lancashire, where the
potatoes consumed as "chips" amount to about 69 per cent of
consumption', whereas in London the proportion totalled 10 per
cent.[2] In 1931 an article in the *Manchester Guardian* pointed to 'the
growing importance and popularity of fish and chip shops, which this
year took 60 per cent of the fish (excluding herring and mackerel)
landed in this country and which will probably increase next year'.[3]
In 1931 the official Sea-Fish Commission for the United Kingdom
accepted the existence of 25,000 shops in the country, with an average
annual turnover of between £1,000 and £1,500.[4]

By the late 1940s and into the 1950s the number of fish and chip
shops began to decline. By this time, official figures emerge about the
numbers in existence that act as a corrective to the estimates provided
by Chatchip. While the Second World War may have had some impact
upon the number of shops in existence, the official survey of working-
class diets suggested that the amount of fried fish consumed per week
actually increased from 1.04 oz (30 g) per head per week to 1.51 oz (43
g) per week, while overall fish consumption rose from 6.61 oz (187 g)

in 1942 to 9.21 oz (261 g) in 1945. Nevertheless, some decline had occurred in the amount of fish caught at the start of the war and would not reach pre-war levels until the end of the conflict.[5] The first official figure we have from the Census of Distribution in 1950 suggested that there were 17,216 establishments in Britain. A decade later R. A. Taylor, in a survey on white fish distribution, estimated that the number of shops stood at 13,750, indicating a significant decline. Nevertheless it meant a ratio of 2.8 shops per 10,000 of the population.[6] In 1956 the White Fish Authority had suggested a figure of 14,834 premises which employed a total of 41,866 people.[7] By this time bleak stories had appeared in the FFR suggesting that as many as 300 shops may have gone out of business in the previous twelve months,[8] although several unofficial investigations carried out by journalists tried to prove the continuing health of the industry. For example, in December 1956 W. J. Cotton, President of the London and Home Counties Fish Friers' Association, declared that 'Fish and Chips Still Reign Supreme' while recognizing that challenges lay ahead, mostly in the price of commodities,[9] a concern which came through constantly in the pages of the FTG and the FFR. In the following year an investigation from a 'Special Correspondent' of *The Times* was published with a headline of 'Fish and Chips Still Frying'. The article nonetheless recognized that changes had recently taken place. It suggested that some artificial growth had taken place in the late 1940s and early 1950s because the Ministry of Food freely granted licences to fried fish shops, which led to closures in the middle of the 1950s because of an artificial boom. By 1957 the trade still used 'more than a third of the total annual intake of white fish – these last year [in 1956] amounted to 865,000 tons – with nearly a million tons of potatoes and about 80,000 tons of fats and oils'.[10]

While concern about the decline of fish and chips continued into the 1960s, the number of shops remained stable before the increasing variety of takeaway foods began to make an impact. In 1964 the annual turnover of fish fryers had reached a total of approximately £100,000,000. They may have used about 1,000 tons of fish each working day and a similar amount of potatoes, making the industry important to both sea fishing and potato cultivation.[11] In 1964 the FFR claimed that: 'Fish is eaten regularly by more than 90 per cent of Britain's population, and the average yearly consumption is about 22 lbs. [10 kg] per head.'[12] But four years later, Sir Louis Chick, Chairman of the White Fish Authority, asserted that: 'Britain ate less fish last year – about 1 lb. [450 g] per person less than in the previous three years.' He put this down to 'changing habits and social standards', including 'watching television at home' which he claimed meant that many families 'no longer nip out to the fish shop round the corner'.[13]

But the zenith of the fish and chip trade lasted for most of the twentieth century. While some decline may have occurred during the 1950s and 1960s, it still remained the most important 'take-away' food for this entire era when it essentially had few, if any, real rivals. From the 1970s the situation would change, although the trade declined gradually. Fish and chip eaters consisted of a fairly reliable group of the working classes who could purchase this cheap food instead of cooking at home, therefore setting the takeaway trend which would continue into the 21st century.

While many of the consumers of fish and chips may have come from the working classes, the owners often remained one step above them on the social scale, and often did not live in the same areas as their customers. Taking the twentieth century as a whole, we can identify three types of businesses in the form of family-owned shops and restaurants, mobile vans and chains. The first of these have predominated throughout the last 100 years, but mobile deliveries have always existed, while chains took off at the end of the twentieth century.

The small, family-owned business has remained most typical throughout. During the interwar years, while an overall decrease had occurred in the number of retail outlets of all kinds, fried fish dealers had actually increased. Evidence of the importance of small businesses is supported by the fact that between 500,000 and 600,000 shops existed in the country during the 1920s and 1930s, or one for every fifteen to eighteen families, suggesting a thriving small retail trade sector.[14] If we accept Chatchip's assertion that the 25,000 fried fish shops in the early 1920s provided direct employment for 75,000 people, this meant that just three people on average worked in each shop, a figure confirmed by the official White Fish Authority survey in 1954 which suggested that, out of the 14,834 fried fish premises which existed in Britain at the time, 7,824 employed fewer than three people, while only 643 employed more than six.[15]

Throughout the twentieth century those who considered opening up a fried fish business could obtain support from a whole range of avenues, including the NFFF and its publications. Between 1921 and 1922 Chatchip published 25 articles in the FTG, subsequently issued in book form, in which he went into meticulous detail about all aspects of establishing a shop. The advice focused upon: the extent and opportunities which existed for opening the shop; the selection of suitable sites; the layout of the shop; the equipment; and the selection of potatoes, fish and the 'minor materials of the frying trade' such as salt, vinegar and peas.[16] In the following decade H. T. Reeves published an even more detailed account of every aspect of the fish and chip trade which required two volumes and 431 pages.[17]

The interior of a 'Modern Frying Establishment' from the 1930s.

Chipping in the 1930s.

As members of the self-employed petty bourgeoisie running small businesses with small profit margins, fish fryers committed themselves to their shops. One account from 1970 pointed out: 'The work is hard and often unpleasant; the hours of work are far from attractive. Rarely are you finished before midnight, and, unless you are careful, you take a fairly ripe smell of fried fish home with you.'[18] Joe Pieri, whose family took over a business in Glasgow in 1933, wrote that 'We had to work hard in the new family shop . . . We closed on Sundays but the remaining six days of the week demanded unremitting hard work. The day started at six o'clock in the morning, when I accompanied my father to the fishmarket.' When they returned to the shop 'the real work of the day' started, which included washing, peeling and chipping – 'either by hand with a knife or by means of a heavy guillotine-type potato cutter which required considerable strength and stamina to operate' – a 'few hundredweight of potatoes', followed by the preparation of the fish, which allowed an afternoon break. The shop opened for business at 4.30 pm. At the peak of the trade in the 1950s 'we could go through a ton of potatoes and about 20 stone of fish' on a Saturday.[19]

However, one article in the FFR from March 1960 claimed that 'A Frier's Life is Quite a Happy One'. The main attraction consisted of self-employment, which meant control over a working life encompassing daily routine and income. Greville Havenhand's account from 1970 claimed that some people viewed a fish and chip shop as a 'goldmine' and wrote of 'the myth of independence' but accepted that 'at least' the fish fryer 'is free to make money by his own efforts and not be held up by the speed of an assembly line or the deliberations of a Whitley Council'.[20]

The small scale of most fish and chip shops meant that they tended to provide minimal profits. In 1935 some fryers could work up to 70 hours per week and exploit the labour of their families, without earning much more than the wage of an unskilled labourer.[21] Nevertheless this era proved one of expansion. Many of the most successful fish fryers had actually gone into business before the First World War and expanded after its conclusion. A. J. Foster, for example, 'took a shop in Humberstone Road, Leicester' in 1912, at the age of twenty. This initially served food over the counter but he and his wife also opened a restaurant and subsequently took over a premises in the same road which could cater for 100 and then 150 people.[22] Nathan Duce, meanwhile, followed in his father's footsteps. After the death of his father in 1899 Nathan helped to run the family business in Watford with his mother and two brothers. The shop faced closure but recovered and during the 1920s he ran several establishments in Reading.[23] The fried fish business also offered opportunities for social mobility for miners, one of the largest male occupational groups in Britain in the first half of the twentieth century. They included James Wesnedge, who bought a shop in 1910, and E. G. Clark, who opened a business in Cardiff after the general strike of 1926.[24]

An article of 1938 in the *Fish Traders' Weekly* focused upon 'Mr Average Fish Frier', one C. Smith, who, contradicting other available evidence for the vast majority of those involved in the trade, owned three shops. He actually came from an educated background, having worked as an instructor in an RAF technical school. Like other fryers, he praised his wife, reflecting the importance of women in these small, family-run businesses.[25]

In 1970 Havenhand gave the example of Ritz Fisheries in Leeds, which seems more like the 'average' shop outlined in statistics. It 'is small, and though it is clean, it has a sort of warm shabbiness that contradicts the goldmine tag'.[26] This quaint portrait contradicts the success stories upon which the post-Second World War fish and chip press tended to focus. These include, for example, Bowers Restaurant in Newcastle upon Tyne, described as having 'a spacious foyer that would not disgrace the newest of super cinemas, impeccably decorated in contemporary style, with built-in floor heating, luxurious settees, aquarium, softly glowing colours, concealed lighting and a great window full of flowers'. The owner of the restaurant, George Bower, another former miner, had actually opened his original business in 1925, which had clearly had much success and therefore necessitated the current move and expansion.[27]

We need to stress how unusual such premises were. The statistics about the size of businesses and the numbers of people involved in them suggest that over-the-counter shops predominated for most of the twentieth century and actually formed the prototype of takeaway which Chinese and Indian establishments would adopt from the 1960s. In 1955 only 26 per cent of fish fryers actually had a restaurant attached to their premises.[28] Chatchip simply spoke of fried fish shops and drew a picture of the floor plan which consisted of a front door, a shop of 15 by 15 feet (4.6 × 4.6 m), a kitchen and pantry, which together took 21 by 12 feet (6.4 × 3.7 m), and a back yard. He also provided plans for several alternatives, which included premises with living quarters.[29] In 1914 he had complained that the majority of fried fish shops 'are very unattractive' and he suggested ways of improving their appearance including tiling the walls.[30] Smith's Supper bar, opened in Green Lanes in Palmers Green in 1932, represented the ideal method of furnishing by this time as suggested in a feature in the FTG, which described the shopfront, the interior decor and the frying equipment.[31] In 1951 a fryer from an unnamed location described the routine in such businesses, which 'ordinarily' ran as follows during the evening:

> First, there is an hour's demand for chips (mostly juvenile), with just an occasional order for fish. Then comes a lull, with an odd visitor now and again, till about 8 o'clock, when the fish and chips supper trade starts and continues till about 9.30, then there is another 'easing off' till the pubs 'turn out' in districts where the closing hour is 10 pm. Now comes another busy spell till about 10.45, when the sparseness of callers indicates it is time to lock up shop.[32]

While this portrait would characterize fish and chip shops in numerous locations throughout the country for most of the past century, by the interwar years restaurants had also taken off, sometimes on a large scale, a trend which would continue into the second half of the twentieth century.[33] By 1933 H. T. Reeves viewed a restaurant as part of any fish and chip shop business, suggesting ways in which to set it out and decorate it.[34] Some of these restaurants existed on a significant scale during the interwar years, following recent trends in other sectors of the catering trade. They tended to lie in southern England, which had emerged from the interwar depression earlier than other parts of the United Kingdom. The Imperial Restaurant in north Harrow provides an example of the most elegant of fish restaurants, actually using 'Japanese oak' throughout. The visitor from the FTG, apart from focusing upon the decor, also pointed out that the takeaway trade remained quite separate from the restaurant business.[35] Meanwhile, the FTG described Morristons in Highgate as a 'super streamlined, up-to-the-minute fried fish shop,

The Imperial Restaurant, 1932.

snack bar and restaurant'.[36] The Commdore Café in Canvey Island, described as 'Modernism in Concrete Glass' and opened by G. Brucciani and E. Biagoni, 'formerly fish caterers in Glasgow', who 'had come south' because of intense competition in the city, had the feel and appearance of an American diner. It could comfortably accommodate 150 people.[37]

A Mass Observation Survey on 'Holidays' from 1941, with a commentary on Blackpool, pointed out that 'fish and chips are easily the most popular meal partaken outside the boarding house. Out of nearly 300 meals observed in restaurants all over Blackpool' 33 per cent included 'chipped potatoes', while 27 per cent included fish.[38] By the 1950s large-scale businesses had therefore reached the North. Bower's Newcastle restaurant operated on a massive scale with a staff of 60 people.[39] Youngman's Fish Restaurant in New Briggate, Leeds, claimed that it could feed 2,000 people per hour. Fiddlers in Cheadle Heath consisted of a takeaway section and snack bar on the ground floor and a restaurant on the first floor which had an 'intimate' atmosphere 'with individual coloured spotlights hanging over each table' and green velvet curtains shading the windows. The clientele of this establishment included both nearby factory workers at lunchtime and also local residents in this Stockport suburb during the evening.[40]

At the end of the twentieth century, as fish and chip shops experienced decline, many commentators focused upon the threat from American multinationals, with their numerous outlets, which would undermine the self-standing, self-employed individual. While dedicated chains remained rare in the earlier days of fish and chips, they certainly existed, albeit on a small scale compared either with the American fast food restaurants or the Harry Ramsden brand at the end of the twentieth century. Of the 16,354 businesses in 1950 'only 442 had more than one establishment and 22 five or more establishments'.[41] Thus a few 'chains' existed on a small scale. For example, Picton's owned two restaurants in Reading and Margate in 1927. The latter was a huge establishment 'capable of seating 700 people at one time' while the Reading branch could hold 200.[42] Some firms involved in catering more generally opened fish and chip businesses such as Blackpool Caterers Ltd which, in 1936, established the Wallgate Fish and Chip Restaurant and Snack Bar.[43] In the 1960s Jack Cohen opened the Quality Fish Bar in Finsbury Park which he viewed as the first in a chain. Similarly Ernie Beckett and J. G. Sprott 'inaugurated' a 'northern chain of restaurants' in Cleethorpes in 1966.[44] Neither of these significantly expanded, however.

Chains therefore remained untypical, as the fish and chip shop usually consisted of a small, family-run business without even a restaurant. At the opposite end of the scale, mobile fish fryers, which have also existed for much of the history of our meal, are viewed with suspicion by the established trade because of their potential ability to take away customers in any number of locations. On the one hand, we might see the origins of these fryers, like their stationary brethren, in Mayhew's street sellers. On the other, a specifically mobile range had come into existence in the form of John Rouse's 'Dandy' from 1880, drawn by horse and cart. By the interwar years mobile restaurants had come into existence in which the frying and serving of fish and chips occurred. Stanley Bays established a fleet of four mobile fish restaurants in Bedford, which he named the Frying Squad, each leaving a depot at 4 pm and covering about 40 miles each before returning at midnight. The mobile business reached a peak in the Second World War and its aftermath, partly because fish did not face rationing after 1945, and partly because evacuees demanded their staple food. In the early 1950s the Morris car company constructed a mobile, motorized fish and chip shop. These businesses operated both in remote areas and in those where local councils did not grant licences to stationary businesses.[45]

Whatever the size of the fish and chip business, owners could receive advice from a range of sources, which helped the growth and survival of the trade. The first consisted of the bodies which represented the fish fryers, above all the NFFF, which not only offered advice but also made representations to government about a variety of issues affecting its members including the price and availability of raw materials, in particular fish and potatoes. While the organization has held an annual conference for much of its existence, it also operates a network of local bodies covering much of the country. At its peak it may have had a membership of 100,000.[46]

The equipment available helped to perpetuate the fish and chip trade because a whole range of companies, which had first emerged by the end of the nineteenth century, continued to provide the necessary tools for anybody wishing to establish a business. Over the course of the twentieth century this apparatus changed as a result of evolving technology and fuel supplies.

Frying Squad, Bedford, 1936.

The NFFF headquarters in Leeds, 2013.

In the early 1920s Chatchip produced articles on all the equipment the fryer needed as well as the variations available. The frying range proved central. In addition to discussing whether or not the range should use gas, electricity, coal or coke, Chatchip also listed a whole series of other points which fryers should take into account when purchasing their equipment, including control of smoke and smell, ease of cleaning and use, but also 'attractive appearance' because it 'will be in many cases, the most prominent piece of the shop furniture'.[47] Chatchip also pointed to the development of potato peeling and chipping machines evolving from a 'potato-scraping dolly', essentially a wooden stool with attachments, to a series of large-scale peelers.[48] Other pieces of equipment included knives for cutting and boning fish, the chip warmer and the fish drainer.[49]

A whole series of companies had evolved for the purpose of supplying equipment to the fish and chip trade from the end of the nineteenth century. By 1937 at least 28 had emerged, concentrated mostly in Lancashire and Yorkshire, a trend which would continue, so that in the 1960s sixteen firms existed within a 50-mile radius of each other. By this time most fryers would have their ranges tailor made for their premises.

During the course of the twentieth century technological developments clearly meant changes in the equipment available to fryers. Power supply played a significant role in the changes. Gas became

The latest potato
peeling machine
in the early 1920s.

increasingly important from the 1930s and had come to dominate after the Second World War, fighting off the challenge of electricity mostly thanks to its cheaper price. Chippers, meanwhile, which had started off as manual in the 1870s, had become electrical by the 1960s. Ranges changed partly as a result of evolving styles but also because of the increasing use of stainless steel.[50]

Infrastructure, labour and entrepreneurship form the background for the evolution of the fish and chip meal itself. The statistics for the type of establishments which existed point to the fact that most of those who ate it did so at home, even though sit-down snack bars and restaurants emerged during the 1920s and '30s. By the early 1920s the standard components of the meal had become firmly established not only in the form of the battered fish and fried potatoes but also the method of frying and the use of salt and vinegar, as well as the availability of side dishes, including peas and meat pies.

Plaice proved the most popular fish for much of the nineteenth century although other species increasingly came into prominence.

A 1920s frying range.

As the twentieth century progressed cod, followed by haddock, became the most popular fish as a result of their increasing availability due to improved fishing and distribution methods. Regional variations appear to have emerged by the 1930s with hake dominating in Wales and skate in London. By the end of the 1960s these variations appear to have changed, partly as a result of shortages. Other popular fish have included halibut and, reflecting the nineteenth-century origins, plaice and sole.[51] Chatchip suggested using a whole range of species including cod, haddock, pollock, whiting, hake, gurnard, sole, plaice and halibut.[52] H. T. Reeves provided a commentary upon all of these fish. He described cod as 'almost indispensable' as it will 'give the utmost satisfaction', although he outlined the benefits and taste of most of the fish he considered.[53] Ultimately, the key issues in the choice of fish, apart from availability and therefore price and, to a lesser extent, taste, consisted of its usefulness for frying which has meant that herring and mackerel have never succeeded because of their oiliness. This explains the importance of white fish. Despite the fact that the fish and chip trade had evolved as a result of the availability of fresh fish, by the post-war years some fryers simply bought it frozen as a result of further evolution in the ice trade.

The other key ingredient was the potato, which could also be purchased ready chipped and frozen by the 1960s, although most chip-shop owners resisted this.[54] No such innovations had yet surfaced when Chatchip advised his readers to 'remember that a business is built up mainly on reputation', meaning that the fryer must take care in selecting the best potato, focusing upon those 'which will have the least possible amount of waste, be economical in its absorption of fat during the process of cooking, and when cooked be both palatable and digestible'. He advised his readers to buy potatoes according to the seasons of early, second early and late, and specified the varieties within each.[55] Reeves, meanwhile, wrote that 'chip-frying must be considered an art' in which the choice of potato suitable for this method of cooking played a large role. 'The advisability of endeavouring to preserve uniform production and colour with fried potato-chips cannot be stressed too strongly.'[56] As an article in the FFR from March 1950 pointed out, apart from the selection of potatoes, the temperature of the oil played a central role, as did the maintenance of the temperature.

The attainment of perfection did not lie simply in the frying process but also in the selection of the frying medium, which varied from one shop to another often based upon regional preferences. From the later nineteenth century and into the interwar years, cotton seed oil had established itself as an important frying medium. The main alternatives in the first half of the twentieth century consisted of lard and dripping, although fryers also used other vegetable oils including groundnut oil, rapeseed oil and coconut oil. Both Chatchip and Reeves could see the relative merits of each of these different frying media.[57] By the 1950s an article in *The Times* could claim that: 'In the north dripping is mainly used for frying, and elsewhere groundnut, cottonseed, and palm oils.'[58] This pattern appears to have become established by the 1930s when the 'Northern men fry the fish in dripping, but the southerners prefer nut oil.'[59]

Chatchip and others also investigated the 'minor materials of the frying trade' which Chatchip described as 'minor in volume only'. These included flour, where he advised his readers that: 'It is very little use the fish frier being careful as to the quality of his fish if he is not also careful as to the quality of the flour he uses for his batter.' He advised against the use of 'cheap and dark flours'. He also gave hints on the use of different types of vinegars in the form of wine, malt, cider, sugar and wood, pointing out that: 'Most respectable friers now use pure malt vinegars diluted with water.'[60]

As the twentieth century progressed fryers increasingly sold other products in addition to fish and chips. The earliest to make an appearance consisted of peas, which may have its origins in Mayhew's pea soup sellers of the middle of the nineteenth century.[61] Chatchip regarded peas as a 'profitable commodity' which he claimed 'scores of friers in parts of the country where peas have not usually been purveyed by the trade have added to their menu' upon his recommendation and which he asserted 'had been welcomed and appreciated by their customers'. Chatchip stressed the use of marrowfats or, what would come to be known as, mushy peas, perhaps an adaptation of Mayhew's pea soup.[62] One Shropshire fryer actually started selling both peas and beans in 1920 because of a shortage of potatoes and found that 'they have gone very well'.[63] Another article from the early 1920s recommended marrowfats and claimed that peas had become especially important in Lancashire.[64] The county seems to have maintained its status as the centre of pea consumption into the 1950s and 1960s, although by this time their popularity had also spread to Yorkshire. In 1958 a Lancashire firm produced 2,000,000 disposable cups which could hold peas, '95 per cent of which went to the fish and chip shops of Lancashire and Yorkshire'.[65] Although hot peas 'have been a stock line in the fish and chip shops in some areas for several years . . . the speed and convenience of easy proportioning in special paper cups with lids has meant increased sales and profits for those already selling peas'.[66]

Other foods also made their way into the fish and chip shop menu, although as late as 1956 there were 'thousands of establishments where 95 per cent of the "over-the-counter" sales are in fish and chips and the other 5 per cent in such sidelines as peas and beans, bottled sauces and pickles, mineral waters, cigarettes and even lolly-pops and ice cream'. The article in the FFR which made this assertion suggested the sale of sausages, either battered or not.[67] By this time pies had also taken off, especially in Lancashire,[68] although they would subsequently spread to the rest of the country. They had actually emerged earlier. An article in the *Manchester Guardian* of 9 September 1936 asserted: 'In the North it has for a long time been the custom for the suburban swain to round off his evening's entertainment of his beloved with fish and chips, or pie, chips, and peas for a change.' A survey 'at a typical chip-shop next door to a typical pub in a working class district' on one day in 1943 pointed out that 105 customers purchased steak pies while 425 bought fish.[69] Nevertheless not all Northern fryers offered pies at this stage. In May 1941 one shop in Blackpool did not serve them, although peas certainly proved a popular line.[70]

While the overwhelming majority of people who ate fish and chips and the various accompanying side dishes purchased them outside the home and ate them in a restaurant or brought them home, recipes from twentieth-century cookbooks suggest that some people cooked the dish at home. A book on *Fish Cookery* issued by the Ministry of Food in 1948 suggested a variety of ways of cooking fish including frying. It offered four possible coatings including 'thick batter', made from '4 oz. flour, 1 egg, fresh or reconstituted, salt and pepper, milk or water to mix (approx. 5 tablespoons)'.[71] Meanwhile, a book compiled by the Good Housekeeping Institute included a recipe for 'Fried Fish in Batter' with accompanying photograph served with 'potato chips'.[72] But while these mass audience cookbooks contained such recipes, other fish cookery volumes did not.[73]

Decline

Fish and chips in Britain therefore reached its zenith in the earlier decades of the twentieth century, when a whole series of statistical sources point to its popularity, especially amongst the working classes. Although signs of decline surfaced during the course of the 1960s, partly as a result of the arrival of Chinese and Indian takeaways, this decline would become more visible from the 1970s as these two cuisines increasingly gained a foothold in the high street and the homes of British consumers. At the same time the spread of American-style fast food also threatened the fortunes of Britain's fryers. Although diversification forms part of the history of the fish and chip shop in Britain, this diversification increased further in the final decades of the twentieth century as fish fryers tried to compete with the arrival of American fast food and other new takeaway foods, including kebab shops, run by immigrants from Cyprus and Turkey. In some cases something of a blurring of boundaries has occurred so that takeaways which primarily sell other products, especially kebabs and burgers, also supply fish and chips as one of many menu choices. The dish has also moved outside the chip shop, not only into these other takeaways, but also into mainstream restaurants as a core menu choice, especially on Fridays, as well as into the home, as ready-made frozen fish and chips hit the supermarket shelves. The other significant change in recent decades consists of the increasing importance of chains, which had never played a significant role in the earlier decades of the twentieth century, but became more important towards its end, partly as a reaction against the American chicken and burger franchises. The evolution of Harry Ramsden's epitomizes these developments but a series of smaller chains has also evolved.

Table Indicating the Decline in the Number of Fish and Chip Shops and Restaurants

Year	Real or Estimated Numbers
1921	25,000
1950	17,216
1960	13,750
1977	11,000
1992	9,500
2003	8,600

Sources: FTG, 2 April 1921; FFR, October 1954; R. A. Taylor, *The Economics of White Fish Distribution in Great Britain* (London, 1960), pp. 141–2; Acumen Marketing Group, *A Report on the Take Away Food Market in Britain* (London, 1978), p. 4; MINTEL, *Eating Out 1992* (London, 1992), p. 2; *Observer*, 19 January 2003.[74]

The issue of the decline of fish and chips remains complex. One statistic which would confirm this fall consists of the reduction of the number of fish and chip shops in the country, although even here a steady decrease has occurred so that fish and chips seems to have retained its position as Britain's most popular takeaway. However, articles regularly appeared in both the fish and chip press, mainstream newspapers, government reports and research carried out by private retail research organizations which tried to analyse and explain the decline in the number of fish and chip shops.

The above table suggests that there was a gradual decline during the course of the twentieth century. Such statistics point to the success of Indian and Chinese restaurants, which took off from the 1960s, and the rise of American fast food, especially in the form of Kentucky Fried Chicken and McDonald's, which started to make their presence felt during the course of the 1960s and 1970s respectively.[75]

Nevertheless fish and chip shops did have some success in fighting off competition from both the Indian and Chinese takeaways and U.S. multinationals. In 1971 Britons spent '£130 million a year on fish and chips, equivalent to the expenditure in restaurants and take-away shops on all foreign foods combined . . . Chinese restaurants account for about £30 millions of turnover, Indian about £20 millions, and all other foreign restaurants about £80 millions.'[76] Four years later an article in the *FTG* pointed to 3,750 Chinese restaurants and takeaways with an annual turnover of £27 million compared to 12,000 fish and chip shops and restaurants with a turnover of £170 million. The article also mentioned the arrival of Kentucky Fried Chicken and claimed that fish and chip shops remained 'dominant in the north and Scotland, while English and foreign takeaways are heavily biased towards the south of England'.[77] At this time 'British fish and chip shops get through 2,000 tons of potatoes and 1,000 tons of fish' on a daily basis.[78] By 1978, 32,500 catering and retail establishments sold takeaway food worth £480 million during 1977. Fish and chips remained by far the most important with over one-third of the market at 11,000 establishments, with the closest rival described as 'cafés'. By this time some of these fish and chip shops and restaurants owned by immigrants also sold Chinese food and kebabs as a menu choice, while chicken, hamburgers and pizzas had made their way on to the menu as well.[79] Another survey, using a different methodology, claimed that fish and chips accounted for 43 per cent of takeaways sold in 1981.[80] Fish and chips remained most popular with groups lower down on the social scale, although people of all age groups consumed it on a regular basis.[81]

Ten years later fish and chips still retained its position, even though some significant inroads had been made into its market share. But one American survey claimed that 'traditional chip shops still have a 25 per cent share of the $1.2 billion fast food market.'[82] In 1992 MINTEL, the market intelligence organization, published a detailed report on dining trends in Britain called *Eating Out*, which suggested significant decline in the position of fish and chips, although it also emphasized the surviving popularity of the dish. This pointed to '127,000 businesses trading in the catering sector' which included pubs, making up the largest percentage of businesses at 33, although 'fish and chip/takeaway restaurants' came second with 24 per cent. In addition, they still accounted for 9,500 of the 31,500 takeaway businesses in the UK, making them the most popular in terms of outlets, although market share (15 per cent) lay behind sandwiches (26) and

A 1960s cartoon demonstrating anxiety and pride at the presence of newly arrived Indian and Chinese takeaways.

hamburgers (18). By this time, not only had hamburger and fried chicken chains established themselves, so had pizza restaurants. Nevertheless, in terms of turnover, fish and chips had grown together with other types of takeaway foods. At the same time fish and chips continued as the most popular fast food in the UK in terms of the proportion of the population that ate it, a fact that remained true for all age groups and all regions of the UK.[83] But decline continued into the following decade. In 2003 while 50 per cent of the British population ate fish and chips once a month, only 14 per cent did so on a weekly basis. Nevertheless, in 2009 fish and chip shops still took up 10 per cent of the British potato crop.[84] By 2012 MINTEL had grouped fish and chip shops together with kebab shops as a category. Using this description, this takeaway proved the second most popular after 'ethnic', which consisted of 'Chinese, Indian, Thai, Japanese, Mexican etc.'[85]

As a result of the threat of the multinational and the Indian and Chinese takeaway, and partly driven by new technology, a series of changes have taken place in the fish and chip trade over recent decades. The first of these consists of ownership, since chains of varying sizes have emerged, although they still own a minority of fish and chip shops; a space still remains in British society for self-employed small businessmen, as epitomized by the emergence of Chinese and Indian takeaways since the 1960s.[86]

By the late 1970s only two companies owned more than twenty outlets each in the form of Friar Tuck and Seafarer. The former, owned by Rank Hovis McDougall, counted 23 shops in Greater London, while the latter, owned by Associated Fisheries, controlled 22 outlets, including the Harry Ramsden label. In fact, several chains had seen a decline in their outlets during the course of the 1970s. Six other groups controlled a total of 59 shops in 1978. But continuing the patterns of much of the twentieth century, a survey of seventeen shops from that same year found that sixteen of them employed less than five staff.[87] Part of the growth which took place in chains did so as a result of the takeover of already existing establishments. Associated Fisheries, for example, purchased Moores Fish Restaurant in Coventry in 1970.[88] By 1985 its Seafarer outlets existed 'from Leeds in the North, through to Wolverhampton and Coventry in the

Midlands, to Canvey Island in the South'.[89] Seafarer had actually begun as early as the middle of the 1960s with ambitions to establish a national chain similar to Wimpy, the first hamburger franchise in Britain, but this never materialized for a series of reasons, including the complexity of producing fish and chips and the raft of planning regulations that affected this dish compared with other takeaway products. At the same time, chains like Seafarer emerged at a time when the appetite for the dish witnessed decline in contrast to the interest in newly arrived foods originating in Asia and the USA. Furthermore, while some small businessmen appreciated the support which they obtained as franchise holders, others felt it limited their independence.[90] A series of other short-lived chains also emerged during the 1970s and 1980s. These included the Hungry Fisherman and Mr Chippy, owned by Westbourne Caterers with seventeen shops in London and the southeast in 1976. Reflecting the triumph of big business in late twentieth-century Britain, these shops appear to have fallen prey to Manor Caterers in 1985, ultimately owned by Rank Hovis McDougall, which meant that Manor operated 44 outlets in the south and southwest. Hugh Duncan and Peter Lipscombe established the Fish'n'Chick'n franchise in northeast London during the course of the 1970s and 1980s. At the same time Nordsee, which owns a chain of fish restaurants in Germany, also entered the British fish and chip market, but this particular enterprise appears to have been short-lived.[91] By the early 1990s ownership and branding of chains took a different shape. Crispins, now owned by KC Restaurants, operated just twelve outlets, down from a peak of 45. Merryweathers, Super Fish, Mr Cod, Nordsee and Harry Ramsden's controlled a total of just 31 shops between them.[92]

Harry Ramsden's, which has gone through various ownerships, has actually proved the most durable and successful of all. Originating in Guisely near Leeds in 1928 and established by its eponymous owner, it claimed to have become the biggest fish and chip shop in the world. In 1972 Associated Fisheries took over this location and marketed the restaurant using a series of statistics which augmented its status. Although Ramsden's began to branch out during the course of the 1970s and 1980s, an important turning point came in

A branch of Harry Ramsden's in Euston station, London.

November 1989, when it underwent flotation on the London Stock Exchange, a move masterminded by John Barnes, former managing director of Kentucky Fried Chicken, which resulted in a significant oversubscription of shares. Its expansion initially remained limited, with fifteen UK restaurants by 1996 together with others in Jeddah and Singapore. But by 2003 it operated 157 outlets, either directly owned by the company or franchised. These included restaurants, takeaways and 'express' outlets, although the number of outlets had declined to 30 by 2012.[93]

Ramsden's has therefore operated upon a significant scale, which, however, remains far behind the 1,000 McDonalds restaurants, 600 Kentucky Fried Chicken outlets, 400 Burger King diners and 286 Pizza Express pizzerias, which existed in Britain in 2000.[94] It also means that the overwhelming majority of the 8,000 fish and chip shops remain small, family-run businesses, continuing the traditions established from the end of the nineteenth century and resembling the 12,000 Chinese restaurants and takeaways and 9,000 curry houses which existed by about 2000,[95] which used the fish and chip business as their model.

In 1971 the *FTG* published a series of articles on the fish and chip trade in Manchester, which involved interviewing owners. For example, they spoke to Mr and Mrs E. E. Pratt, proprietors of the Regal Fish Bar in Baguley, who had worked in the trade for many years and continued to use fresh fish, in contrast to many businesses which had adopted frozen fish. Mr Pratt prided himself on the quality of his product, but also recognized that the success of his business found partial explanation in its location, near three schools, and in its recent refurbishment. Whitakers Fish Bar in Cheadle Hume, meanwhile, sold fresh fish, including scampi, together with fresh chicken, pies, a variety of peas and beans and curry sauce. The owner, Joseph Houghton worked in the shop with his wife, two sons and shop manager.[96]

Over the following decades we can see the patterns of these restaurants, following those established at the end of the nineteenth century, repeated throughout the country, as articles published in the fish and chip press indicate. While some businesses remained small in scale, others, again following long-established patterns, catered for dozens or even hundreds of customers. A sampling of the articles illustrates the essential nature of the fish and chip shop and restaurant as a family-run businesses, varying in scale, but also points to the menu change which has taken place.

By the end of the twentieth century some restaurants had a long history and often remained in the same family, passed down from father to son. For example, in 1990 George Leonidou was running the Seafresh Fish Restaurant in Wilton Road, near Victoria bus and coach station in London, together with his brother Mario, following in the footsteps of their father who had originally established a fish and chip shop in the 1940s. George claimed to have worked his way through the business, having assisted his father as a child. While the restaurant sold chicken, sausages, saveloys and spam fritters, it concentrated upon fresh fish, including *kalamari*, and also had an alcohol licence. This business actually employed twenty full- and part-time staff.[97] Meanwhile, by 2003, the Tutners had been working in the fish and chip trade in Spalding for 90 years, although the site of their business had gone through several relocations. By the early 21st century the fourth generation found themselves working in the restaurant, which, by this time, could cater for 140 people in an air-conditioned environment, as well as providing takeaways.[98] This sort of continuity actually provided an important transfer of expertise through generations which, in some cases, allowed the establishment of small, family-run chains in a particular area. Thus the Long family had originally opened a fish and chip shop from the 1930s, and by 1999, the grandson of the original owner had set up his sixth establishment, all in the southwest, in this case in Salisbury.[99]

Despite the longevity and expansion of some businesses, some individuals have moved into the fish and chip trade for the first time in recent decades, as their predecessors did a century earlier. Some have previous experience as small-business people. For example, Huw and Sarah Jones, previously in the 'fruit and veg' trade, opened Finnegan's Fish Bar in Bridgend in 2001, employing twelve staff and opening seven days a week. As well as having 'an extensive menu, ranging from the traditional fish & chips to vegetarian, chicken, curry and low fat dishes', it also offered a delivery service.[100] John Rogers, who had inherited a dairy farm, opened the Jolly Rogers Fish Bar in 'rural Devonshire' in 2004 after marrying and having children with his wife Kelly. Profits from his farm had declined to virtually zero and he also wanted to spend more time with his family. In fact, both Kelly and her mother had previous experience working in her parents' fish and chip shop in Blackpool. Her mother also helped to establish the new business, which partly survived from the local tourist trade.[101] Other individuals had little or no business experience. Alan Smith opened a hot dog stand after facing redundancy and subsequently established a fish and chip shop along with his two brothers-in-law in Aviemore Shopping Centre during the 1980s.[102] Steve and Kathy Goodacre purchased their local fish and chip shop in Peterborough in 1976, which meant selling their terraced house. Steve had previously 'worked in accounts'.[103]

As in the earlier part of the twentieth century, some mobile fish and chip businesses survived, although they continued to attract criticism from the NFFF.[104] A new development, perhaps forced upon the trade by the practices of pizza firms in particular, consisted of home delivery. Thus Matt Bedford, owner of Fishtastic in Peterborough, decided to add this to his business which meant purchasing bags from Pizza Equipment Ltd to keep the food warm, as well as hiring three drivers because of the level of demand.[105]

Fish and chips has also gone upmarket in recent decades, epitomized above all, perhaps, by the opening of a fish and chip restaurant by the celebrity chef Rick Stein in Padstow in 2004, alongside his other, even more upmarket establishments in this Cornwall seaside resort.[106] This trend started with the publication of *The Gourmet's Guide to Fish and Chips* in the 1960s.[107] The idea of consuming our dish with wine has also recently become popular.[108]

Further diversification has characterized the evolution of fish and chip shops over recent decades. During the 1970s, the FTG pointed to 'pies, pasties and chicken portions'. By this time several companies provided a range of side dishes, especially for fish and chip shops. Baughan's Food Ltd, for example, 'worked very closely with the fish trade to develop products that are not intended to replace fish sales, but rather to attract those customers who on a particular occasion prefer an alternative to a fish meal'. These products included frozen saveloys, beefburgers and meat pies. Zee Fraiza Speciality Foods in Watford produced pizzas and 'boil in the bag' Chinese food.[109] In 1985 Richard Bennett's fish and chip shop and restaurant in Ramsgate, which prided itself on using local produce, sold 'cod, plaice and haddock fillets, clam fries, seafood platter, prawnburgers, scampi' as well as 'a selection of meat courses such as chicken (traditional or southern fried), Daloon rolls and beefburgers, as well as sausages, pies and pizzas'.[110] A survey from 1978 found diversity not simply in the whole range of products sold but also in the different type of fish which included cod, haddock and plaice, as well as scampi, fish fingers, skate and hake.[111] Despite concerns about supplies of cod, this still remains a mainstay of the fish and chip trade, with increasing numbers of purveyors sourcing it responsibly, although a wide variety of new specimens have entered the menu such as pollock fished in Alaska and catfish farmed in Vietnam.[112]

Technological change has also taken place since the 1970s, including the importation of Dutch-style ranges from the 1980s, resembling those used in other fast food operations, separating fish frying from chip production.[113] In the same way in which the trade adopted major pieces of equipment used in the takeaway trade generally, it also took on packaging used in other sectors, including polystyrene, although at the beginning of the 21st century some companies continued to produce bags and boxes specifically for fish and chip shops.[114] Although the businesses which sold the best quality dishes always used fresh products, many shops have increasingly used not only frozen sidelines but also frozen fish and chips.[115] By the end of the 1980s fish fryers had become professionalized with the introduction of a City and Guilds 'Fish Frier Practice' certificate. This not only taught people how to chip and fry but also how to run a business.[116]

Despite the fact that itinerant fryers have always existed, owners of
shops and restaurants have always viewed them as a threat,
as this British cartoon of 1949 suggests.

FRYING TIMES
TUES TO SAT
11 A.M. TO 1.30 P.M.
7.30 P.M. TO 11 P.M.

COD	FROM	6½p
HADDOCK		9
PLAICE		9
SKATE		11
COD ROE		5
BEEFBURGER		6
CORNISH PASTIE		5½
CHIPS		4
PEA FRITTER		2
FISHCAKE		2½
SAUSAGE		2½
CHICKEN		15
COTTAGE PIE		14

Fish and chip
bill of fare,
1960s.

As well as a meal eaten in a restaurant or purchased in a takeaway, fish and chips has also become available frozen so that people can simply heat it up. In one sense this remains in keeping with the origins of the dish as a method of saving time on cooking, although the taste remains inferior to that purchased hot and deep fried from a specialist.[117] For those who wish to approach the quality of the product freshly cooked, recipes in books and newspapers have become normal, especially those focusing on British food,[118] although variations on the original theme have emerged, as evidenced by Pru Leith's 'Oriental Fish and Chips'.[119]

Transformation and Survival

Fish and chips has therefore survived the entire course of the twentieth century and beyond. The raw statistics for the number of fish and chip shops point to decline, as do other figures which have tracked the regularity of fish and chip eating in Britain. Yet, for almost the entire twentieth century, from its heyday before the 1960s, until the 1990s, it remained the most popular takeaway, despite the arrival of Chinese and Indian cuisine and the invasion of American fast food. We could offer a number of explanations for this continued popularity including, perhaps, the fact that, as the original takeaway meal in Britain, it proved difficult to shift, no matter what competition came along. Just as importantly, it has also remained relatively cheap, keeping with one of its original attractions, comparing in price with other takeaways which also use genuine ingredients such as fried chicken, pizza, Indian and Chinese food and kebabs, although slightly more expensive than American beefburgers. The basic and ultimately nutritious nature of fish and chips (despite recent health concerns, which some snooty middle-class commentators emphasized from the early twentieth

Training at the NFFF headquarters in Leeds, 2013.

century) has perhaps also aided its survival.[120] While technological developments mean that fryers can buy frozen and cut chips and prepared batter mixes, the meal remains healthier than virtually any other takeaway, especially from those shops and restaurants which carefully source their fish, potatoes and other ingredients and remain true to the advice of Chatchip and Reeves. On the other hand, perhaps it could be said that pure conservatism explains the survival of fish and chips, although this would seem difficult to prove in view of the proliferation of restaurants and takeaways with origins around the globe which have thrived in Britain since the end of the Second World War. As a result of these changes, fish and chips has become just one of many available to Britons, especially in the takeaway sector.

While the meal itself may remain similar to the original dish outlined by Chatchip and Reeves, adaptation has certainly taken place. We would expect this in the nature of the restaurants and shops, which evolved over the century, encompassing new technological developments in the frying process. We can almost see fish and chips as a symbol of change in British society, even though, at its essence, it remains constant in the form of fried potatoes and battered fish. Change happened around it, in the methods of frying, the methods of selling and the ways of preparation. At the same time the fish and chip shop has managed to survive by bringing in new products, some of which originally, in the case of peas in particular, either complemented the dish or acted as a substitute for chips, although, increasingly, new products such as pies, sausages, pizza, kebabs and even Chinese food, have acted as an alternative or substitute for the fish or the whole meal.

On a symbolic level – and from a purely culinary point of view – fish and chips has many meanings. The nature of the business also tells us something about British society. From its beginning the fish and chip shop has offered an outlet for enterprising individuals to establish a small firm. Many of those who entered the trade, just like many owners of Indian restaurants at the end of the twentieth century, simply opened a shop or restaurant as a business opportunity, perhaps one in which they imagined easy

George's Fish Bar, Hornsey, London, illustrating the
increasing diversification of fish and chips, 2013.

profits (although the reality did not always match the dream, as
business failure also occurred). Nevertheless, as the narrative above
has demonstrated, the history of fish and chip enterprise provides
many examples of people who, if not quite beginning in rags and
not quite ending in riches, have run viable businesses. By the end of
the twentieth century many of the most successful of these enterprises
involved people with a family history in fish and chips. Newcomers
still enter the trade for the first time, but success for such people may
have proved more difficult because of increasing competition from
other forms of takeaways and American corporations. By the
beginning of the 21st century fish and chip chains became
increasingly visible for the first time, especially in the form of Harry
Ramsden's. Despite this, family-run fish and chip shops continue to
survive, indicating that a space still remains in British society for

the small entrepreneur. While fish and chips has increasingly come to symbolize Britishness, it has also provided an indication of the success of small enterprise.

THREE

Britishness

Fish and chips has developed a range of identities since its genesis in the middle of the nineteenth century. When fried fish first surfaced in popular consciousness it became associated with the Jewish community in Britain. More specifically the smell of fried fish became the smell of the inner-city ghetto in which many Jews found themselves living in Victorian Britain, especially in the East End of London. However, as the nineteenth century progressed, and fish became combined with chips, the dish became associated with the working classes, as is evident in the few sentences about it written by Dickens and the larger contribution on the subject by Mayhew, as well as in newspaper articles, which often focused on the health threat of fish and chips. In the latter part of the twentieth century our dish became associated with Britishness. While this development may have origins before the Second World War, fish and chips has increasingly become labelled the food of the British.

What follows will precisely illustrate the various links of our dish with Britishness, beginning with the nineteenth-century association with poverty and proceeding to the contemporary connection with national identity. While the latter evolves from the views of both British and non-British writers, the fish and chip trade has played a central role in this construction. At the same time, when fish and chips has moved abroad, it has represented the food of the British. In some cases this happens as a result of marketing yet, at the same time, it has also become associated with the British abroad, including holidaymakers.

The Food of the Working Classes

John Walton emphasized the link between fish and chips and the working classes, describing it, at one stage, as having an 'identification . . . with slums and slum-dwellers, with unpleasant smells and dubious hygiene and with the encouragement of "secondary poverty" through injudicious domestic budgeting by unskilled housewives'. These ideas were 'widely shared among middle-class observers, journalists and social commentators'.[1]

While such ideas survived into the twentieth century, their origins lie in some of the earliest references to the dish. We could argue that fish and chips never escaped from its association with the squalor described by Mayhew and Dickens. While the middle-class commentators who reinforced this image from the late nineteenth century and into the twentieth may not have had much consciousness of such associations, these early references served as the keystone for the connection with poverty and the working classes.

If we return to Dickens, the location of the fried fish warehouse mentioned in *Oliver Twist* lies precisely in the type of slum area for which the adjective 'Dickensian' emerged, as it lay in a 'dismal alley leading to Saffron Hill' with 'filthy shops'.[2] An extract from *Household Words*, which Dickens edited, almost mirrors the above:

> Near a shabby market, full of damaged vegetable stuff, hedged in by gin-shops – a narrow, slimy, ill-paved, ill-smelling, worse-looking street, the majority of the houses private (!) but with a sprinkling of marine shops, rag-shops, chandlers' and fried-fish warehouses, low-browed, doorless doorways leading to black rotten staircases, or to tainted backyards, where corruption sits on the water-butt, and fever lives like a house-dog in the dust-bin, with shattered windows, the majority of them with a sort of desperate resolve on the part of the wretched inmates to clutch at least some wandering fragment of pure light and air: this is Gibbet-street.[3]

While set in late eighteenth-century France, the reference to chips in the Saint-Antoine suburb of Paris in *A Tale of Two Cities* has a similar association with poverty. The sentence in which the word chips appears for the first time runs as follows: 'Hunger rattled its dry bones among the roasting chestnuts in the turned cylinder; hunger was shred into atomies in every farthing porringer of husky chips of potato, fried with some reluctant drops of oil'. Immediately afterwards Dickens writes of:

> A narrow winding street, full of offence and stench, with narrow winding streets diverging, all peopled by rags and

nightcaps, and all smelling of rags and nightcaps, and all
visible with a brooding look upon them that looked ill.[4]

This description could appear in virtually any Dickens novel about
any range of subjects and we might argue that we are reading too
much into the association of fried fish and chips with poverty. On
the other hand, most of the potted histories of the dish begin with
the extract from *Oliver Twist*, even though such histories do not
stress poverty.

Similar comments apply to Mayhew's references to fried fish and
its purveyors who 'live in some out of the way alley, and not infre-
quently in garrets'. Mayhew also asserted that: 'Their residences are
in some of the labyrinths of courts and alleys' in several locations in
central and east London. He focused especially upon the smell of the
fish, which anti-Semites also stressed. Mayhew wrote that:

> among even the poorest class there are great objections to
> their being fellow-lodgers, on account of the odour from
> the frying. Even when the fish is fresh (as it most frequently
> is), and the oil pure, the odour is rank. In one place I visited,
> which was, moreover, admirable for cleanliness, it was very
> rank . . . The garments of the fried-fish sellers are more
> strongly impregnated with the smell of fish than were those
> of any 'wet' or other fish-sellers whom I met with.[5]

This association with smell begins with the first appearance of fried
fish and continues into the twentieth century.

Dickens and Mayhew simply represent the best known writers
who make the link between the poor and fish and chips, in this case
in its primeval form (before our two components married), while
also, certainly in the case of Mayhew, remaining reasonably objective
and not (too) derogatory. However, newspaper and magazine articles
for much of the nineteenth century portray similar images, often in
much stronger and more negative language. The themes which
emerge in a range of narratives include the close link between fish and
chips and the working classes and the issue of smell.

An article in *Chambers's Journal* from 15 March 1879 on 'Cheap Shops in London' mentioned

> fried fish shops – and you must go to the East End to taste fried fish to perfection – where you can have a good fill for about twopence. There are thousands among the wretched classes who have no plates or knives, and who if they could not buy something ready cooked from such shops, would have nothing cooked at all.

Meanwhile, George Gissing's novel *Workers in the Dawn* opens with a description of 'Market-Night' in Whitecross Street, in which poverty forms a major characteristic of the activity. The narrator follows 'a little girl, perhaps four years old, the very image of naked wretchedness' trying to sell salt.

> Follow her, and we see with some surprise that she runs to a near eating-house, one of many we have observed. Behind the long counter stand a man and a woman, the former busy frying fish over a huge fire, the latter engaged in dipping a ladle into a large vessel which steams profusely; and in front of the counter stands a row of hungry-looking people, devouring eagerly the flakes of fish and the greasy potatoes as fast as they come from the pan.[6]

H. D. Lowry, in a piece on 'The Mysteries of Walworth Road', painted a similar picture:

> The first few minutes of a Saturday night spent in the Walworth Road are filled for the visitor with confused impressions of crowded pavements, of people almost fighting to secure bargains at the butchers' shops and of the evil odours of flaring paraffin lamps and innumerable fried fish bars from which there comes a constant stream of people bearing pennyworths of fish in bits of newspaper.[7]

Poverty in London,
1899, sketch.

Such negative perspectives focusing on the poverty and the eating habits of the working classes contrast with the description given by Olive Malvery a couple of decades later, who viewed fish and chips as a way in which the poor could make ends meet.[8] In the extracts quoted above the link with poverty comes through clearly.

Other late Victorian commentators did not produce such essentially derogatory discourse. An article on 'Street Cookery' in London from 1872 simply reported in a matter-of-fact way that 'Fried fish are in greatest demand on Saturday evenings, when they are eagerly bought by workmen and their wives going to, and coming from, the market.'[9]

The association of fish and chips with the working classes and poverty continued into the twentieth century. George Orwell made this link in both an objective and more judgemental manner. In *The Road to Wigan Pier*, a passage describing the economic depression and its consequences during the 1930s points out that 'You can't get much meat for threepence, but you can get a lot of fish and chips.' On the other hand, an essay written after the Second World War described fried fish as: 'The habitual supper of the poorest of the working classes'.[10] Robert Roberts, meanwhile, in a study of his home town of Salford in 1971, wrote that 'in the early years of the century only the "low" in the working class ate chips from the shops. Good artisan families avoided bringing them, or indeed any other cooked food, home: a mother would have been insulted.'[11]

Smell and health remained two of the key elements in negative stereotypes of fish and chips. By the end of the nineteenth century those who did not follow bylaws which prevented fish frying at home, could face prosecution. Thus in 1897 the Medical Officer of the Sanitary Committee of Middlesbrough Corporation pointed out that

I have inspected the premises No. 68 Russel-street, Middlesbrough, used as a fried fish shop, and the process of frying fish was in progress at the time. I also inspected the houses on each side of No. 68, and I have no hesitation in

Fish frying in progress, 2013.

certifying that there is a nuisance owing to the offensive effluvia
and ill-smelling gases given off in the course of the fish-frying
now being carried out in the front parlour of No. 68 Russel-
street. The premises were only built for a residence, and have
not been properly adapted for such business and the people
living in the houses on each side are being subjected to an
intolerable amount of distress and inconvenience.[12]

The introduction of further legislation and an improvement in the
quality of equipment for extracting smells meant that odour became
less of an issue, but an article in the *Manchester Guardian* of 3 August
1929 mentioned it, especially in reference to 'passers-by' during a
'heat wave'. One of the most evocative and nauseating descriptions
of the smell of fish and chips has nothing about frying fumes. In her
account *Ladybird Lane* (1962), Sarah Francis, who taught in 'a school
of Educationally Sub-normal Children, in the slums of a city',
remembered visiting, with her colleague Mr Landon,

> large buildings with perhaps twelve or fifteen rooms, with
> one family living in each room. Babies and small children
> played with potties full of urine and excreta underneath
> tables covered with a hotchpotch of buckets, milk bottles,
> bread and indescribable remains of food. Apathetic mothers
> leaned back in chairs or propped up doorways.[13]

She continued:

> In some rooms there was no furniture except a table and a
> couple of chairs. In addition, there was a sickening, vaguely
> familiar smell, which made me want to vomit. At last I
> asked Mr Landon about this overpowering odour which we
> encountered in almost every building.
>   'It's mainly the smell of fish and chips and urine', he
> answered. 'The women don't do much in the way of wash-
> ing, and if the children wet their pants they hang them up
> to dry. The same thing happens with the babies' nappies.

As for washing the floors, well, your guess is as good as mine as to how they are cleaned. Fish and chips are the main food of this community, hence your smell.'[14]

This extract perfectly sums up the middle-class image of fish and chips and its association with the poor, showing that the attitude persisted as late as 1962.

It also hints at the link with bad nutrition. During the nineteenth century the connection essentially focused upon the fact that bad cooking practices could cause sickness. One plaintiff claimed that the smell of fried fish from a shop opened next door to his house actually made him so sick that he had to move.[15] More recently a connection has developed between fish and chips and obesity. For example, a report by 'Experion, the data analysts' from 2004 pointed to a 'north–south divide on obesity', asserting that 'high levels of obesity are strongly linked to class'. The report asserted that in areas with a high percentage of council housing, such as Hull, 'Parents don't educate their children about having a healthy diet. They have old fashioned diets: the traditional diet in that area is fish and chips. We found ten fish and chip shops in the centre of Kingston upon Hull, whereas there was none in Kingston upon Thames.'[16] Fish and chips, like other fast foods, has become an important focus in the healthy eating debate in Britain in recent decades, even though a portion of fish and chips remains healthier than many of its fast food competitors, so long as the serving is not excessively large.[17]

The Construction of a National Icon

Despite the fact that the image of fish and chips as the food of the working classes has survived until the present, as the twentieth century progressed fish and chips increasingly became associated with Britishness, a development which lends itself to a variety of explanations. In the first place, with the arrival of overtly foreign foods during the 1950s and 1960s, especially as sold by Italian, Chinese and Indian restaurants, British public opinion increasingly became conscious of its 'own' food and found that, in the simplistic stereotypes which surround popular discussions of food and its link to national identity, Britons fell back on what appeared to be the national dish. Fish and chips had, by the twentieth century, replaced the earlier culinary symbol of Britishness that was roast beef.[18] Towards the end of the twentieth century cookbooks increasingly appeared upon ethnic lines. Those which focused upon British food almost invariably contained a recipe for fish and chips. Globalization, especially as manifested in the obvious manner of the supermarket shelf, also stressed ethnic differences between foods.[19] Meanwhile, the link between fish and chips and Britishness spread beyond Britain, not only because foreigners increasingly viewed it as the quintessentially British dish but because whenever it made an appearance abroad, it symbolized the British, either because they ate it outside the UK or because companies marketed it in that way.

While the link between fish and chips and Britishness solidified in the years since the 1950s, it has its origins in the 1920s and 1930s. Before this time, when foods generally had no assigned nationality, neither did fish and chips. However, during the late 1920s and early 1930s a few newspaper articles begin to make the connection with Britishness. For example, the *New York Times* in 1928 wrote that

A window poster stressing the Britishness of fish and chips, 2013.

'England's hot dog is "fish and chips"'.[20] In the following year a letter to the *Hull Daily Mail* declared that: 'Fried fish and chips are a national institution. What would thousands of people do in Hull for supper if it was not for fried fish shops?'[21] Two years later the fish trade began to jump on this bandwagon when Sir John Marsden, president of the British Trawlers' Federation, declared that 'the one thing that could properly be called a national dish to-day was fish and chips.'[22]

Before 1945 these sorts of statements remain isolated. But from the 1950s cookery books, the press and marketing by the fish and chip trade and its newspapers stress the connection with Britishness. A major turning point in this process came with the publication in 1953 of Philip Harben's *Traditional Dishes of Britain*. Harben had become one of the first television celebrity chefs in Britain and could therefore bring his ideas to a mass audience. He became one of the first to overtly and simplistically make the link between food and nationality. The chapter titles of his book list the stereotypical stalwarts of the British diet, including 'Cornish Pasty', 'Bakewell Pudding', 'Yorkshire Pudding', 'Shortbread', 'Lancashire Hotpot', 'Steak and Kidney Pudding', 'Jellied Eels', 'Haggis', 'Clotted Cream' and 'Fish and Chips'. Harben tells us that: 'This is a book about the fine food of Britain and of some of the associations – historical, geographical, traditional – that go with it.'[23] The central chapter is the one on fish and chips. Harben begins:

> What is the national dish of Britain? This book is full, of course, of national dishes which are all popular favourites; but what is *the* national food? The teeming millions of Asia subsist mainly on rice. Macaroni in its various forms is the staple diet of Italy. Germany and sausages are almost synonymous. When you think of Scotland you think of porridge. What, then, is *the* national dish of Britain? The Roast Beef of Old England? Not a bit of it! The answer is: Fried Fish and Chips.[24]

Harben's argument here, while rather simplistic and generalizing, partly revolves around an important truth in the sense that fish and chips had become the staple of the English working classes playing, he argues, the same role as rice in Asia. Harben asserted, as John Walton would do later in the century, and as Chatchip had done in the 1920s, that 'this dish, and this custom, has played a seriously important part in our national nutrition and economy.'[25]

As the century progressed both cookbooks and other publications built upon Harben's views, without referencing him. A Time-Life International book from 1970 on *The Cooking of the British Isles* almost repeats Harben, in a tongue in cheek manner, by asserting that: 'The Americans eat hamburgers and apple pie; the French eat all manner of things in sauces . . . the Germans eat sauerkraut and sausages . . . Such generalizations have, of course, more than a grain of truth in them.' While the English 'always' eat roast beef on Sundays, 'every other day of the week they eat fish and chips'.[26]

John Walton's finely researched volume on our dish also stresses connections with Britishness and, above all, the working classes. While he did not overtly focus upon national identity, he clearly writes about the food of the British. Reviewers of the book, many of whom produced sneering commentaries, did, however, engage with this theme, especially an assertion he made that fish and chips saved Britain from defeat in the First World War.[27] Meanwhile when Mark Petrou, a fryer himself, published his more populist volume, he subtitled it *A National Treasure*.[28]

By the 1960s cookbooks had become increasingly drawn along ethnic lines, following the arrival of 'foreign' takeaways, meaning that just as volumes on Italian, Chinese and Indian food emerged, so did books on British food in response, which usually contained a recipe for fish and chips. This is true of books by Gary Rhodes and James Martin, for example.[29] The multi-authored *Great British Menu* from 2006, which works according to regional origins and cooks from particular areas, actually lists 'Classic Fish and Chips' under Wales, although it could presumably have found itself in any region used by this book.[30] Heston Blumenthal's *In Search of Total Perfection*, which tackles foods with origins from all over the world, describes fish and chips as 'virtually Britain's national dish'. The recipe, in keeping with others in Blumenthal's book, involves a strange range of ingredients and equipment. The former include white rice flour, honey, vodka, lager and turbot, while the equipment includes a 'soda siphon and CO_2 charges, digital probe, deep-fat fryer, atomiser (optional)'.[31]

At the same time as cookbooks perpetuated the idea of fish and chips as a British national dish, so did newspapers and magazines, both British and international. The *New York Times* has for decades regurgitated the classic stereotypes about the British and their food, in which fish and chips plays a central role. In the late 1950s and early 1960s the paper repeated their earlier description of the dish as the equivalent of hot dogs and hamburgers in the USA, indicating its acceptance of food as a signifier of national identity. One article on the first Wimpy Bars in Britain carried the title: 'U.S. Hamburger Finally Arrives in the Land of Fish and Chips'.[32] Another stated:

> Fish-and-chip stalls are as much a part of the British scene as hot dog stands in the United States. The crucial ingredients are cod, fried potatoes and the wrapping paper in which the two companion delicacies are carried away from stall or shops.[33]

At about the same time, another article entitled 'Fish and Chips Imperilled by Potato Shortage' carried stereotypes such as the following:

> For generations, Britons have stopped at their local chip shops at lunchtime or on their way home from work and emerged with the staple wrapped in a sheet of newspaper. They can also eat it on a plate in the shop, but most do not because they say it tastes better on newsprint.[34]

Such stereotypes continued late into the twentieth century so that one article carried the title (using a cockney accent reminiscent of Dick Van Dyke in *Mary Poppins*): 'Fried and Salty, Yessir, Matey, but Truly English'. The slightly less condescending article asserted: 'Fish and chips endures as England's original hot fast food, a quintessential institution.'[35] Using Hollywood stereotypes from the other end of the social scale, another piece carried the title 'It Takes a Stiff Upper Lip to Love Fish and Chips' and began with another much repeated assertion that 'Fish and Chips are to the British what hamburgers and fries are to the Americans. So every American who wants to go native will try fish and chips at least once on a visit.' The rest of the article described, in less stereotypical language, the best fish and chip shop in London and the way to eat the dish, as well as the best side dishes. Nevertheless the writer, Marian Burros, gives the impression of an intrepid explorer, driven around by a taxi driver, sampling the food of the natives and concluding that 'even when fish and chips are perfectly prepared, according to the English tradition, they are as bland as nursery food.'[36]

Not all *New York Times* articles on British food are so condescending. A piece entitled 'A Defense of English Food – Some of It, Anyway', proceeds, after an opening paragraph ridiculing foods with names such as toad in the hole, bubble and squeak and bangers, 'Laughter aside, England is the homeland of at least three of the most interesting foods ever devised – roast beef with Yorkshire pudding, steak and kidney pie, and fish and chips.'[37]

President George W. Bush followed the instructions of the *New York Times* on a visit to Britain in 2003 when, accompanied by Tony Blair, he visited the Dun Cow pub in Blair's constituency in Sedgefield, County Durham, where, 'Mr Bush, a teetotaller, opted for a non-alcoholic lager to accompany fish and chips, with the northern variation, mushy peas.'[38] In this sense both the British prime minister and the U.S. president happily played their roles in an unequal partnership in which the former offered the latter the stereotypical American image of British food.

British newspapers have also focused upon fish and chips as a national dish, especially in articles which have concentrated upon its history. In 2010 both the *Daily Mirror* and the *Daily Express* celebrated the 150th anniversary of the dish. The former began its piece by stating that: 'After fuelling the industrial revolution and sustaining morale through two world wars, Britain's favourite meal is 150 years old.' The *Daily Express* article, meanwhile, opened:

> Fish and chips is a dish more loved by this nation than any pie, pasty or Marmite soldier. It is as much a part of our national fabric as Morecambe and Wise and the monarchy. The takeaway that we sprinkle with vinegar is up there with a pint, a cuppa and Corrie.

These pieces operate in a celebratory manner, rather than the condescending tone to be read in many *New York Times* articles.

The article in the *Daily Express* actually based its assertion upon an initiative by the Department for Culture, Media and Sport which asked the public to nominate 'Icons of Britain'; fish and chips came first.[39] This followed a comparable survey carried out in 2004 and sponsored by Tanqueray Gin, which reached similar conclusions. Questionnaires asking 'what was the most distinctive symbol of being

Tony Blair and George W. Bush waiting for fish and chips in the Dun Cow pub, Sedgefield, County Durham, 2003.

A fish and chip shop in Edmonton, Canada, 2012.

British' found that fish and chips came joint first, along with roast beef and Yorkshire pudding. A piece in *The Times* by Robin Young, who reported this survey, perceptively observed that: 'Once the British were identified by those distinctive characteristics the stiff upper lip, a willingness to queue and ineptitude at foreign languages. Now, though, it seems that we are what we eat.'[40] Another survey carried out by the InterContinental Hotels Group four years later produced similar results, although on this occasion fish and chips came first on its own.[41] Young's assertion makes an important point about the way in which, during the course of the twentieth century in particular, foods have increasingly become linked with national identity.

At the same time as media and popular discourse perpetuated the Britishness of fish and chips, so did the trade itself, partly as a marketing tool to distinguish the meal from the competition of curry, Chinese food, pizzas and beefburgers. But even as early as 1952, before any other takeaway had made its presence felt, the NFFF

A British woman serves up fish and chips in this poster from 1976.

issued posters and window cards describing our dish as 'Britain's favourite food'.[42] Similarly, a campaign from the late 1960s ran a series of adverts under the heading of 'The Truth about Fried Fish', followed by sixteen points detailing its virtues, mostly along health grounds. The first of these stated: 'Fish and Chips as a meal was Britain's first convenience food, and remained the top favourite for 100 years.'[43] In the 1970s another campaign using the slogan of 'The Great British Dish', came with a poster of a large-bosomed lady in front of a Union flag carrying a plate of fish and chips. A firm called Kiltie, which 'supplies a wide range of fish and other frozen foods to fish friers, fishmongers and caterers throughout the country', actually lay behind this campaign.[44] At the beginning of the 21st century, again with the use of the Union flag, and stressing the nutritional benefits, another campaign proclaimed: 'Fish and Chips: The Grrrrreatest of all British Inventions'.[45]

The trade certainly believed its own propaganda and marketing. From as early as July 1953 the *FFR* asserted that: 'Fish and chips are not only a British meal in the sense that they are so very popular in this country; they are also produced from British materials.' Three years later the *FTG* stated: 'Notwithstanding the doleful reiteration of the pessimists, that fish and chips as the national dish has had its day, the trade advanced with the times in 1955, and stands more securely than ever – the people's favourite food.'[46] In 1980 the *Fried Fish Caterer* declared that fish and chips 'are part of the British way of life'.[47]

The trade newspapers also tried to stress the cultural significance of fish and chips. History has acted as one vehicle for this process enabling these publications to use every conceivable anniversary to emphasize Britishness. An article from the June 1965 edition of the *FFR* on '100 Years of Fish and Chips' carried the subtitle 'From Humble Origins to a National Asset' and then presented a potted history of the meal. A review of John Walton's book in the *FFR* ran under the title 'Patriotic Dish for Posh and Poor'.[48] During the 1960s the same newspaper also stressed the role of fish and chips in British life by interviewing celebrities who ate it, including The Beatles, who apparently claimed that 'Our success depends on this handy meal.' John Lennon, 'the leader of the group', stated: 'We're in and out of fish and chip saloons all the time.'[49] By the end of the 1990s the trade even had 'its own official poet' in the form of 49-year-old Peter Street 'named by the Poetry Society as the first chippy laureate' and receiving 'a £1,500 grant from the Arts Council Lottery Fund' with the aim of 'reflecting' the 'history and significance of fish and chips' by using 'the medium of poetry'. His work included 'Mates':

Last night's newsprint,
Tasting of chips – wet,
Tanner a bag.

Contemporary
culinary
nationalism,
2013.

FISH
&CHIPS

The Nation's Favourite
What other food will give you energy, proteins
to build muscles, vitamins and minerals
to keep you healthy and still have less fat
than most meats and meat products?
Fish and Chips *The Grrrrreatest of all*
British Inventions

Folded artistically,
To stop all that pea juice
Dipping onto best hand-me-downs.

Walking home after the last bus
With mates you confessed everything to,
Good friends, together
In a meeting place
Smelling of fish and chips.[50]

The poem essentially romanticizes a lost, working-class northern
childhood, in which, in this case, the smell of fish and chips has a
positive connotation. It uses the derogatory comments which greeted
the dish a century earlier in a positive fashion, pointing to its progress
from a marginalized food of the working classes to one which now
stood at the centre of British life. This inclusion into the mainstream

receives further confirmation from the fact that in 2008 the NFFF 'were asked to provide all things appertaining to making a fish and chip shop in the grounds of the British Embassy in Guatemala for the Queen's Birthday Party'. In the following year the British Embassy in Rome 'wanted to convert a function table at the grounds of Villa Wolkonsky (the ambassador's residence) into a mini fish and chip shop'.[51]

Fish and Chips Abroad

John Walton almost lamented the fact that our dish 'failed to become one of the great British cultural exports of the ages of Industrial Revolution and Empire'.[52] While fish and chips had become a symbol of Britishness by the second half of the twentieth century, this identity did not simply become established within the country's borders. Despite Walton's statement, fish and chips has had some success outside Great Britain, whether in former British colonies or in places where Britons take their holidays, especially in the Mediterranean, where fish and chip eating and Britishness have become almost synonymous.

Ireland appears to regard the dish as its own in the same way as Britons do. An article in the *Irish Times* from 3 November 2011 entitled 'How Fish and Chips Enriched a Nation' began 'There's nothing more Irish than a fish supper', although the piece points out that Italian immigrants first established the dish in Dublin, a fact also mentioned by Walton.

The dish in Ireland essentially fits into the history of the country as part of the English-speaking world,[53] which would also explain the presence of fish and chips in the white colonies. By the late 1930s the dish had also made some impact on Canada. 'In Montreal, Toronto, Winnipeg, Vancouver and all the larger cities, there are dozens of fried fish shops, particularly in industrial suburbs.'[54] Businesses survived into the post-war period and the present day.[55] Fish and chips seems to have reached Australia by the end of the nineteenth century as a result of the efforts of an English immigrant. It would expand gradually during the course of the twentieth century. Priestland ate in several establishments there during the 1960s, although he remained lukewarm at best about the food that most of them served. In 1980 David Thatcher visited several businesses in Australia which used a variety of fish, including plaice, whiting, flounder and red snapper. Indeed, Australia has offered opportunities to Britons who wanted to migrate and establish fish and chip businesses, including Louise and Adrian Warner, who moved to the country in 2006. In 2009, using the most blatant of English stereotypes, they opened a shop called Chumley Warner's Traditional Fish and Chips in Brisbane, which attracted both British and Australian customers. Those who have eaten here have stressed the British experience. One Australian couple asserted that 'Our weekly visit is the highlight of our English fix', while a British diner wrote: 'Proper traditional fish and chips with all the trimmings. I just wish it was closer to home. The only place in Australia I believe, where you can get a proper steak and kidney pud with soggy salt n vinegar chips.'[56] The dish has also reached South Africa and New Zealand. According to informants of Gerald Priestland in the 1960s, 'it's just like home' in the latter.[57] In South Africa the frying trade appears to have taken off as the result of the efforts of an immigrant from Cardiff who opened a business in Port Elizabeth in 1926 and quickly increased this to six, which resulted in others, including at least one Dutchman, following his lead. By the 1940s at least one South African cookery book included recipes for frying fish in a variety of batters.[58]

Fish and chips reached the Continent in the 1920s. Since that time both Britons and Europeans have stressed its Britishness, either positively or negatively. In the autumn of 1923 the 'Great Fish Week at Boulogne' included stands attempting to popularize our dish, though with little success.[59] However, something of a fried fish boom appears to have taken place in Germany in the second half of the 1920s when as many as 300 shops sprang up, including at least 24 in Berlin, thirteen in Hamburg and eight Bremen. A German Fish Friers Association, based in Bremerhaven, existed until the 1960s. Although a decline in numbers had taken place by the 1930s, between 80 and 100 fried fish shops still existed in Germany in the early 1950s.[60] By the 21st century the Nordsee fish restaurant chain often

Fish and chips in
New Zealand,
2012.

ran promotions featuring fish and chips, which always stressed
Britishness, while other smaller companies have followed suit,
including Klassigs. Unlike practices in Britain, both the fish and the
chips had been precooked and would be warmed up by deep frying
again. In 2012 Nordsee sold 'Fish and Chips, klein und gross' advertised
in English as 'real love' and 'Very British', although the dish itself
consisted of small pieces of Alaskan cod resembling chicken nuggets
served with tartare sauce and thick chips packed in a paper cone
with newspaper print on the outside.[61] By this time a few businesses
had also appeared in France including one run by Bill and Joyce Hughes
in Paramé, Brittany, in the early 1990s, whose clientele included locals,
members of the British community in the area and tourists from
Canada, Scandinavia and Belgium.[62] Several establishments in Paris have
also served fish and chips, always stressing its Britishness. These have
included restaurants which overtly marketed themselves as selling
British food, some of which faced hostility in the French press because
of the association of Britons with bad cooking.[63] Further afield, Ahmet
Suleymangil, the 'manager of a successful chain of restaurants in Turkey
. . . opened the first British-style fish and chip restaurant in Istanbul',

called King Fisher, which imported many of its ingredients and its equipment from the UK.[64]

In the USA fish and chips has had to fight against British stereotypes, although some businesses have willingly used them as marketing tools. For example, in New York 'the Chip Shop resembles a theme park, with its Mini Cooper delivery vehicle.'[65] In 1960 'The English Fish and Chip Shop', also in New York, placed printed circulars near the front door, which stated:

THIS IS HOW YOU DO IT
When Visiting England

There then followed a list of ten instructions, which included: 'ask the shopkeeper for "one and six and a tanner mate" (i.e., 1*s*. 6*d*. fish, 6*d*. chips)'; 'walk in busiest street and every third step take a dip into newspaper'; 'when greasy right hand brings out nothing from lucky dip, screw up newspaper into a ball, drop ball at feet, and kick ahead for half a mile'.[66] Despite the partly self-perpetuated stereotypes, fish and chips may have had more success in the USA than any other

Fish and chips in Berlin, Alexanderplatz, 2013.

Cooper's Fish and Chips Store, New York, 1936.

country outside Britain. As early as 1899 fried fish shops appeared in the Upper West Side in New York. As in Britain at the same time, these businesses 'are a boon to the woman who doesn't want to cook, or who for some reason or other cannot do so at a particular time'. Every evening 'poor women' waited outside the shops 'for a specially fried order'.[67] But these shops seem to have been short-lived. In the early twentieth century only isolated businesses appear to have established themselves. These included the Fish and Chip House in Seattle at the end of the First World War and Cooper's Fish and Chips Store in New York in the middle of the 1930s. The latter claimed it could sell 1,000 meals per day.[68] Something of a boom occurred in the 1960s when, imitating the growing fast food businesses such as McDonalds and Kentucky Fried Chicken, a series of chains developed in the form of H. Salt, Arthur Treacher's, Alfie's, Chappy's and Long John Silver's, founded by a combination of Englishmen and Americans and often run as franchises. For example, Haddon Salt (i.e. H. Salt) from Lincolnshire established a chain of more than 400 outlets, while Carl B. Zucker from Texas ran Alfie's. In addition to these chains some self-standing small businesses had also emerged whose names worked on predictable stereotypes including Union Jack Fish & Chips, Olde English Fish n' Chips, Yorkshire Fish &

Chips Shoppe and HMS Cod. Some new chains emerged during the course of the 1970s including Captain D's, based in the southeast of the country with an Americanized menu which, in addition to fish and chips, included 'shrimp and oyster dinners, catfish, chicken, cheese-burgers, and giant burgers'. By the end of the 1970s Treacher's had a total of 153 company-owned and 362 franchise outlets.[69] The chains and franchises appear to have run out of steam during the course of the 1980s, but individual businesses have certainly survived, often but not always playing to British stereotypes. Those that do not include Foley and Son of Worcester, Massachusetts, while those that do include the New York-based shops A Salt and Battery and the Chip Shop.[70] In the land of immigrants where everything, including food, has an ethnic identity,[71] it seems inevitable that fish and chips should play the role of the quintessential British food.

While chains and franchises helped to spread our dish within the USA, Harry Ramsden's helped to make it global; in addition to the branches established in Britain, others have opened all over the world. By 1995 the company ran businesses in Hong Kong and Melbourne and by 1998 it had opened branches in Singapore, Jeddah and Dubai. The manager of the last of these pointed out: 'We import everything from the UK – batter, vinegar, the lot – and locals go for it all now.' To add to the English theme, 'the surroundings replicate those of every other Ramsden's restaurant, right down to the checked tablecloths.'[72]

When venturing abroad fish and chips therefore has a culinary identity as clear as any other cuisine which makes its mark outside the country in which it emerged. In the same way as pizza and pasta have become identified with Italy, 'Chinese' food with China and curry with India, so fish and chips has become the symbol of British food in an international context. It certainly does not have the global appeal of pizza and pasta or 'Chinese' food. Neither has it undergone a culinary transformation once it has left home, unlike the three types of cuisine mentioned above,[73] even if some variations have occurred. However, as the manager of Harry Ramsden's in Dubai pointed out, the dish eaten in Dubai is identical to that eaten in one of the company's shops anywhere else in the world. Despite the authenticity of fish and chips on a global scale, in the sense that even abroad customers

'Traditional' fish and chips are found in eating establishments throughout the world, including George's Fish Bar in Hornsey, 2013.

still eat the fish battered and the chips with salt and vinegar (although the type of fish eaten may differ from that in Britain) marketing and stereotyping has ensured that it remains firmly tied to its British roots.

As many of the stories about the opening of fish and chip shops beyond British shores have indicated, enterprising emigrants have played a significant role in the export of our dish, pointing to the way in which it has followed British people abroad. Some travelling

Britons have also associated fish and chips with the taste of home. In 1966 the Scottish singer Lulu claimed:

> When I was in the States in December doing TV shows and talking over the offers of filming in Hollywood, I made a startling discovery.
>
> They don't have fish and chip shops there. It's their dietary loss, of course. There just are no fish and chip friers on Sunset Boulevard! Now, I ask you! It's no wonder I'll not settle there, is it? [74]

One former Scotland Yard detective from the northeast of England living in Texas associated the dish with the shop from which he purchased it in Durham: 'Of all the things I left behind in England, the thing that I miss the most is Bimbis' fish and chips.' The 'company is blast-freezing a portion of fish and chips to ensure its order remains in tip-top condition' and then sending it out to him.[75] Even more evocatively the BBC journalist John Simpson remembered: 'I was never

Ali Rumsden's in Alhaurin el Grande, Malaga, Spain, run by a British man of Asian origin, *c.* 2000.

aware of the fact that fish and chips played any important part in my psyche until I was in Sarajevo during the siege of 1993.' With food and water scarce, he found himself thinking and talking about food with his companion. 'I just wanted fish and chips. As we drove around in our armoured car I could just taste it, it was so close, and cooked to perfection. The chips were golden and the fish superb.' Simpson actually pointed out that he only ate the dish once a year, 'but it takes me back to my childhood because my father and I used to have fish and chips at the same place a long time ago'.[76]

Communities of Britons abroad have also continued to eat the culinary symbol of Britishness. When Tim Albert visited British immigrants working in Dubai in 1976 he found 'a country club where you can play darts, eat fish and chips and drink English draft bitter'.[77] Similarly, in the reconstructed English villages which constitute army barracks abroad, fish and chips remained widely available together with other British food.[78] The same happens in the ethnically British settlements in Spain where, along with the use of the English language and the establishment of clubs, people have eaten the food associated with home including Yorkshire pudding, fish and chips and shepherd's pie, together with branded products such as Marmite.[79] Majorca has attracted both British settlers and mass tourism from Britain since the 1960s,[80] which has meant that fish and chip shops have followed. For example, Geoff Thomas opened the Codfather in 1993, which served fish and chip shop fare from March to November.[81]

Cyprus has experienced a similar boom in British tourism since the 1960s, which has meant that British food had become widely available on the island. Most of the restaurant owners consist of Cypriots, some of whom have previously lived in Britain and may also have run fish and chip shops. The owner of Erimi's Kitchen, on the old B road from Limassol to Paphos, and therefore off the beaten track and away from the tourist areas in these two towns, had previously owned a fish and chip shop in Coventry, but his new establishment sold kebabs, mezes and 'traditional fish and chips', with menus in both Greek and English.[82]

The Britishness of Fish and Chips

Erimi's Kitchen points to the more complex ethnicity of fish and chips than the focus upon its Britishness might suggest, especially when the origins of owners of fish and chip shops are examined. However, over the last century the dish has increasingly become associated with the British as their national food, especially since 1945. In the period when the meal took off in the decades leading up to the First World War, the identity it possessed, if any, consisted of one associated with poverty and the working classes, which middle-class writers emphasized. By the interwar years fish and chips began to have an association with the British more broadly. But only from the 1950s and beyond does it become the culinary symbol of Britishness as indicated by cookbooks and articles in a wide variety

'Traditional' fish and chips at Erimi's Kitchen, Cyprus, whose proprietors had previously owned a frying business in Coventry, 2007.

of publications and the fact that it follows the British abroad. Even when it does not move abroad, it becomes associated with home, as John Simpson's recollections indicate. On the one hand, the Britishness of fish and chips therefore exists in imaginary, discursive and marketing spheres. While we might suggest that Philip Harben's book plays a key role in a literary sense in establishing the Britishness of fish and chips, the arrival of other forms of takeaways during the 1960s and 1970s forces an ethnic identity upon the dish. In the same way in which curry became associated with India and pasta with Italy, fish and chips became the food of the British because, by the 1970s, all foods needed a nationality, an idea perpetuated not simply by the presence of restaurants on the high street but also by cookbooks, which became increasingly drawn along ethnic lines, and supermarkets, which reproduced takeaway foods according to nationality. Even when fish and chips travelled abroad, it often did so to areas which contained significant numbers of Britons, such as the white Commonwealth or holiday or settlement destinations for Britons such as the Mediterranean coast. When it moved beyond these areas, those who have sold it in the past half century, whether Harry Ramsden's or u.s. chains, have also stressed its Britishness.

Marketing, cookery writing and the fish and chip trade have therefore increasingly stressed the Britishness of our dish since the 1950s. While this forms part of a process of constructing and assigning an identity, the idea of Britishness has much legitimacy because of its origins in Victorian Britain and its role as a staple of the British working classes for much of the past century. However, an examination of other aspects of this dish point to the fact that migrants to Britain have played a significant role in its evolution and survival.

FOUR

Ethnicity

By the second half of the twentieth century fish and chips had evolved into the culinary symbol of Britishness. Such a construction meant ignoring certain realities about the dish and those who sold it. In the first place an examination of the origins of the two components would suggest that they originated outside British shores, so that chips may have entered the country from France, while battered fish had Jewish origins, perhaps dating back to the early modern period. For much of the nineteenth century fried fish was known as the food of the Jews. In fact the vicious anti-Semitic stereotypes which circulated in Victorian Britain assigned the odour of fried fish to Jews. Along with constructed and grossly exaggerated facial features came smell.

While this remained an assigned racist characteristic, fish and chip shop owners have indeed often been members of ethnic minorities. Some Jews certainly did sell fried fish in Victorian London and would continue to do so into the middle of the twentieth century. Italians also played a significant role in the evolution of this trade not only in Ireland but also in Scotland and Wales. Since the Second World War people from the Mediterranean have remained important to the fish and chip trade, especially people from Cyprus, although ownership has become increasingly internationalized in recent decades. While the media and the trade itself feels comfortable in the 'British' identity of fish and chips, the reality remains somewhat different as an examination of the dish's origins, Jewishness and ownership indicates.

The Foreign Origins of Fish and Chips

In the past decade an acceptance has evolved about the fact that the origins of fish and chips may lie beyond British shores, even though suggesting this may still cause surprise in some circles. In 2004 my employer, De Montfort University, issued a press release in connection with my project *Spicing Up Britain*, a book which examines global and migrant influences upon British food. The Press Association became interested in this and turned it into a story about the foreign origins of fish and chips, which led to media attention throughout the world. The *Financial Times* of 9 January 2004 carried an article under the bizarre heading of 'Kosher French Connection with Fish and Chips', while the *Daily Star* of the same morning ran a story under the banner of 'Le Great British Feesh and Cheeps: It's Frog Nosh Claims Prof'. The BBC even asked a representative from Harry Ramsden's fish and chip chain to comment on the story. An official statement declared: 'It's very interesting to hear the professor's findings on the origins of the ingredients that are still, and we're sure will always be, a great British tradition.'[1] The press release also attracted attention among the extreme right in Britain, so that my name appeared on a neo-Nazi website forum, with numerous other public figures, under the heading of 'Know Your Enemy'.[2]

Despite the furore which this story caused, it has resurfaced upon several occasions since that time, suggesting that something of an acceptance of the 'foreign' origins of fish and chips has taken place. On 23 January 2006 Patrick West published an article in the *New Statesman* entitled 'We Didn't Invent Fish and Chips', which asserted: 'England's "traditional" dish is an imported hybrid. It became popular in the late 19th century, when workers decided to marry the Belgian/French custom of frying chipped potatoes with the immigrant Jewish tradition of deep-frying fish in batter.' By 2010 even proud defenders of Britishness such as *The Times*,[3] the *Daily Mail* and the television chef Clarissa Dickson Wright had accepted this position. The *Daily Mail* carried an article with the lengthy title 'The Portuguese gave us fried fish, the Belgians invented chips but 150 years ago an East End boy united them to create the World's Greatest Double Act.' The piece then carried a potted history of fish and chips, claiming that Jewish refugees had originally brought fried fish with them when fleeing the Spanish Inquisition in the sixteenth century, while the origins of chips lay in Belgium.[4] Dickson Wright, meanwhile, points to dishes

> we regard as quintessentially English that are, in reality, recent arrivals. All should be celebrated. Take fish and chips, for example: a resolutely English dish made with potatoes

that came from South America in the sixteenth century and weren't turned into chips until the fried fish that originated with Victorian Jewish migrants.[5]

Despite the shock that greeted my assertion in many quarters, it became orthodoxy within less than a decade, even though neither the original press release nor the newspaper articles which followed provided much concrete evidence.

One constant which remains throughout consists of the Jewish origins of fried fish although, as the extracts quoted above suggest, a variety of stories have emerged to 'prove' its Jewishness. Claudia Roden popularized the idea of the Jewishness of fried fish in her *Book of Jewish Food*, pointing to a Latin text from 1544 written by Manuel Barrano, a Marrano (or crypto-Jew) in England (at a time when Jews could not live in the country), who described fried fish – sprinkled with flour, dipped in egg and then breadcrumbs and then fried – as the favourite dish of his community.[6] An article in a supplement to the *Jewish Chronicle*, celebrating the 350th anniversary of the readmission of the Jews to England, repeated this story while also pointing to the Jewishness of Joseph Malin, who opened the first fish and chip shop in London.[7] A piece in the same newspaper from 4 June 2009 entitled 'Some Like It Cold' reasserted much of this narrative, while also claiming that: 'Fried fish was originally a Shabbath dish which could conveniently be cooked on Thursday or Friday morning, and eaten cold by (southern European) Sephardi Jews on Friday nights or Saturdays', a tradition which the author of the article, Simon Round, claimed his Ashkenazi family of Eastern European origin maintained until the present. Roden made a similar assertion, claiming that:

> Whereas fish and chips became the English national dish, cold fried fish became the most popular method of cooking for the Jews in Britain. My mother-in-law told me that when her family had the fish shop in the East End, they used to fry fish every Friday and distribute it to relatives.[8]

The possibly Jewish Malins in the early 1970s.

Meanwhile a newspaper article from 1868 on a court case involving a Jewish defendant mentioned that before the Passover 'the chief rabbi visited all the prisons and made arrangements for the Jewish prisoners to have Passover cake, fried fish, and oil.'[9]

The classic novel of Victorian Jewish East End life, Israel Zangwill's *Children of the Ghetto*, abounds with references to fish eating whether fried or not. A description of 'high tea' stated that 'in the ghetto' it 'need not include anything more fleshy than fish.' Furthermore

> Fish was indeed the staple of the meal. Fried fish and such fried fish! Only a great poet could sing the praises of the national dish . . . Jewish fried fish is always served cold. The skin is beautiful brown, the substance firm and succulent. The very bones thereof are full of marrow; yea and charged with memories of a happy past. Fried fish binds Anglo-Jewry more than all the lip-professions of unity. Its savour is early known of youth, and the divine flavour, endeared by a thousand childish recollections, entwined with the most sacred associations, draws back the hoary sinner into the paths of piety. It is on fried fish, mayhap, that the Jewish matron grows fat.[10]

Zangwill constructs an almost spiritual link between Jews and fried fish eating, giving it a central place in Jewish cookery and identity. While Zangwill uses it as a positive symbol of Jewishness, many anti-Semites would use it negatively by focusing upon smell rather than taste.

This evidence, some of it personal and some of it impressionistic and second hand, points to the Jewish origins of fried fish. Cookbooks also help to demonstrate the link, especially Hannah Glasse's recipe mentioned in chapter One, suggesting that the cold version has a long history. The Victorian cookery writer Alexis Soyer provided several recipes for fried fish, including one in the Jewish fashion 'which is constantly in use by the children of Israel and I cannot recommend it too highly; so much so, that various kinds of fish which many people despise are excellent cooked by this process'. The process described involved frying in batter. After suggesting the cutting up of halibut and laying it on salt to dry, the fish should be dipped in the batter made of 'two ounces of flour' mixed with water in a 'soup-plate'. Frying should take place in a pan 'with a quarter pound of fat, lard, or dripping (the Jews use oil)'. He suggested eating it with a variety of sauces as well as plain. 'It is excellent cold, and can be eaten with oil, vinegar and cucumbers, in summer time, and is exceedingly cooling.'[11] A contemporary of Soyer, Eliza Acton, provided a recipe for cold fried fish, in this case without batter, in a section of her *Modern Cookery for Private Families* entitled 'Foreign and Jewish Cookery'.[12] Elsewhere, the most famous Anglo-Jewish cookbook of the Victorian age suggested two methods of frying fish, including the 'English Way', while the recipe entitled 'Fried Fish in Oil' involves dipping the fillet in beaten eggs followed by flour 'so that the fish may be covered entirely with it' and then placing in a pan of 'the best frying oil at boiling heat'. The recipe concluded: 'Fish prepared in this way is usually served cold.'[13] If we move forward 100 years to the most famous Anglo-Jewish cookbook of the twentieth century, we find a similar recipe to the one published in the *Jewish Manual*. Florence Greenberg listed four ways of frying fish, including, once again, a method for serving it cold, which involved dipping it in plain flour seasoned with salt and then egg (in that order).[14] While a variety of ethnic groups fried fish,[15] it seems that frying became especially associated with Jews and that the use of batter had a particular Jewish connection, especially when it involved just eggs and flour.

Less evidence exists on the foreign origins of chips, but they may have originally started in France as 'French fries'. Significantly, as we have seen, the mention of 'husky chips of potato' by Charles Dickens is set in the Paris of *A Tale of Two Cities*.[16] It seems that recipes for the frying of potatoes existed in France from the middle of the eighteenth century and into the early nineteenth, therefore predating those found in English cookbooks in the Victorian period, most famously that of Soyer. Again, we might attach significance to Soyer's birth and early life in France.[17]

As a street food, chips appear to have taken off in France during the nineteenth century, perhaps slightly earlier than in Great Britain, and they rose to prominence there during the second half of the nineteenth century, just as in Great Britain. A similar pattern emerges in Belgium, where chips first became popular in the 1840s and had become a widespread street food by the end of the nineteenth century.[18] The assignation of 'French fries' occurred in the USA rather than Great Britain during the nineteenth century.[19] Nevertheless, the recipe in the *Girl's Own Paper* for 'Fried Potatoes' from 31 July 1886 asserted: 'It may be supposed everyone knows how to fry potatoes, but we are convinced that comparatively few know how to fry potatoes after the French method', that is, 'cut lengthwise in finger-shaped pieces'.[20]

It proves more difficult to make connections between the French and the arrival of chips than it does with Jews and fried fish. The missing link here consists of immigrants who could bring over and popularize the produce. As we shall see, Jews appear to have become associated with fried fish both through myth and reality. On the other hand, we do not have the same level of attention devoted to French people in England, even though their numbers totalled nearly 30,000 in 1861 at the time of the first census which asked for respondents' place of birth. This remains lower than the approximately 50,000 Jews who lived in Britain, although these consisted of both immigrants and their descendants. Fried potatoes may have French origins, but there remains limited proof to indicate that they made a journey from France to England with migrants. Part of the problem may lie in the fact that French people in Britain have remained largely absent from the historical record, ignored by both contemporaries and historians.[21]

The Food of the Jews

This contrasts with Jewish people who, before 1945, received constant, mostly negative, attention, representing, along with the Irish, the most visible migrant community in Britain. As a series of historians have demonstrated, anti-Semitism remained part of everyday life, leading to the emergence of a series of stereotypes, some of which originated in the medieval period, while others surfaced with the development of a new strand of this hatred at the end of the nineteenth century. Scholars of anti-Semitism have stressed the way in which hatred of Jews could reconfigure itself and focus upon any aspect of their lives wherever they stood on the social spectrum. The middle of the nineteenth century may represent the period when Jews emerged from the more extreme forms of medieval persecution by finally gaining full civil rights as a result of emancipation, but this did not mean that hostility towards them disappeared.[22] In the early nineteenth century, the period of our primary concern here, one classic stereotype consisted of the inner-city thief and exploiter of children Fagin, in a period where a significant proportion of the Jewish population remained confined to urban ghettos, especially in the East End of London, at least in the eyes of the Gentile majority, even though this represented a period of social mobility for many Jews.[23]

Amongst the anti-Semitic stereotypes which emerged in this period, one even focused upon the food of the Jews, which, until the early twentieth century, resolutely remained fried fish, with a particular focus upon smell so that in the image which would emerge, inner-city Jews both ate and smelled of fried fish. Some commentators even claimed they could sense the ghetto because of the smell which emanated from it. Before this odour became associated with the working classes it had become connected with the inner city and, in some cases, socially mobile Jews. The link between Jews and fried fish becomes clear from an examination of nineteenth-century newspapers and periodicals. The tone of the stories which we discover varies from one to another. Some remain largely factual, others engage with what we might describe as casual anti-Semitism, while still others produce vicious images.

The factual accounts include those covering other issues, which simply mention fish eating in passing. In 1824 we learn of a boxing match between Barney Aaron, 'the light-weight champion of the twelve tribes' and Peter Warren in Colacbrook, 'eighteen miles from London'. The evening before the contest the area around Petticoat Lane in East London 'was occupied in frying fish and cooking other victuals for refreshment on the road' for those Jews who would make the journey to watch Aaron box.[24] Then in 1853 we learn of 'Sarah Lipman, spinster, an ordinary-looking young woman of the Jewish persuasion' who 'was indicted for endeavouring to conceal the birth of her infant child' by burning it. From the reporting of the story we learn that Lipman 'kept a fried fish shop in No. 32, Cable Street, Whitechapel'.[25] Neither of these stories deals to any great extent in anti-Semitic stereotypes, especially the second. They either mention fish frying in passing or in order to set the scene.

We then come to stories which contain either 'casual' or more extreme anti-Semitism. The former do not have any real venom but indicate the widespread nature of this form of racism in nineteenth-century Britain. In such stories, Jewish stereotypes, while present, remain subdued. Although essentially observations of the lives of the London Jewry in particular, they cannot resist the use of stereotypes, which characterize popular discourse about Jews in Victorian Britain.[26] The more overt articles leave us in no doubt about the link between Jews and fried fish.

For instance, a newspaper report of an election for the position of alderman in Portsoken in the City of London from 1844 between 'Mr Sheriff Moon' and 'David Salamons, Esq.', included the following outburst:

We quarrel not with a Hebrew because he holds pork as an abomination (there is the more for those who like it); but because he is a Hebrew. Let him stick to his fried fish, his beard, his old hats, his usury, his gold, his synagogue, his everything that is peculiarly his own, we care not!

This second sentence contains virtually every Jewish stereotype in nineteenth-century Britain including usury, religion, appearance and, central to the whole picture, the consumption of fried fish.[27] In 1848 an article entitled 'A Walk Among the East of London Jews' stated that you instantly knew when you entered a Jewish area because of:

the almost universally-opened windows, by the men and women seated in chairs upon the pavement before their dwellings . . . by the dingy shops of second-hand wares, the clusters of dirty frippery hung from the door posts, the plates of oil-fried fish displayed in the cook-shops and the masses of old iron and fusty rags.[28]

A newspaper article from 1858 provided an account of 'the labyrinth of narrow lanes and alleys collectively known as Petticoat-lane' in East London and described as 'the terra Judaica' on a Sunday. Most of the customers at the market consisted of Gentiles but the street thronged with 'dozens of Jew vendors . . . At every step, we were accosted with invitations in true Hebrew accent to try on coats, waistcoats, trousers, boots, hats, and a brisk trade was going on at every step.' When the writer reached Middlesex Street via Whitechapel he came across, 'lots of fried fish, and to prove its genuineness you could see the little round fat women in yellow dresses, streaked with fishy smearing, frying it might and main'.[29]

Similarly one of the classic accounts of fish frying from the Victorian period, by Watts Phillips, stresses the Jewishness of the women involved. The shop where the business takes place

The late Victorian Jewish East End.

is tenanted by a family of five . . . the heir to the house of Manasseh. The mother, though obese, is comely to look upon, with eyes of melting lustre, and nose, whose size, and lips, whose pulpy fullness, indicate her race . . . With a look that might become the mother of the Gracchi, Rachel stands among her children; only suspending her labours to use the fork as a weapon of offence upon the curly head of her ill-conducted offspring, Jacob, who, hovering about the fragrant heap, is ready to pounce upon the interdicted but too tempting morsels.

The elder daughter of the house stands near her mother, with the face and presence of her namesake Judith . . . Leah, the second daughter, is carefully sewing some tinsel on an old satin slipper, and is singing a popular song to the interesting accompaniment of the frying-pan . . . Sarah, the youngest of the Hebrew Graces, is indulging in a series of skirmishes with the unruly Jacob . . .

Hiss – bubble – bubble – goes the pan, as a fresh shoal of fish plunge into it . . . O, daughters of Judah, even Mr. Spooner will not deny that there is yet one triumph left you – ye fry fish well.[30]

The smell of fried fish indicated the presence of Jews in anti-Semitic Victorian Britain. A visitor to Ramsgate in 1849 wrote:

The first peculiarity that struck me was the strong prevailing smell of fried fish – the very sea seemed so redolent of sweet oil – the land emitted a savour similar to that of a soup kitchen in full operation; while the people who thronged the pier bore unmistakeable evidence of being a Caucassian race. I deemed I had slighted upon some Israelitish colony, that I had entered the land of promise at a period of high festival, and that I should find fried and stewed fish to all frequenters, and that Change-alley and Capel-court, Houndsditch and America square, had poured forth their populations, who all seemed agitated by some unusual excitement. The mystery was soon revealed – the great Rabbi Adler, the high priest, was here on a visit. Salmon had, in consequence, vanished from the stalls of the fishmongers; soles were extinct; but lobsters, and shrimps, and prawns, and crabs, and mussels, being by Levitical law forbidden, their prices rose with a correspondent elevation on the piscatory exchange. Sir Moses Montefiore, the destined Alvator of the chosen race, has here a marine villa, which is reached by a never-ending, still beginning, series of steps, hewn out of the cliff, very properly designated 'Jacob's Ladder'; and here of course wended the chief members of the Synagogue; for albeit Sir Moses is now scattering piastres to the indigent of Damascus, his portals are ever open to his co-religionists.[31]

Meanwhile another commentary on Whitechapel mentions 'a neighbour of mine, of the Jewish persuasion, who smells fearfully of fried fish'.[32] Similarly, and perhaps most bluntly, George Augustus Sala, on visiting the Theatre Royal on Low Lane in 1872, wrote:

There was a representative of one of the Ten [sic] Tribes in every private box; all the money- and check takers were

This is Miss BECKY SOLOMONS at home.　　And this is the beautiful REBECCA at Margate.　　And this is her Pa !　　Ditto.

A Victorian cartoon stressing the Jewishness of fish fryers by using anti-Semitic stereotypes.

process-servers; the wardrobe was supplied by costumiers who carried bags on their backs, and wore three hats instead of one; and the refreshment rooms smelt of fried fish.[33]

The first and third of these extracts prove particularly interesting. Most associations of fried fish link the smell with the Jewish inner-city ghetto. In these two cases the people concerned have moved out of the areas traditionally associated with them, yet the smell remains. It has almost become a racial taint, similar to the anti-Semitic visual stereotypes which focus upon physiognomy. While Jews might move out of the ghetto their appearance and smell will always give them away. These extracts indicate the ubiquitous and changing nature of anti-Semitism in the nineteenth century, which could focus upon both rich and poor Jews.[34]

The focus upon poor Jews received renewed attention in the decades leading up to the First World War due to a significant influx of East European immigrants, who invigorated the east London community. These newcomers faced a new wave of anti-Semitism, which led to the passage of the Aliens Act of 1905, the keystone of modern British immigration control.[35] The old stereotypes about the food and smell of the Jews gained a new lease of life. An article on Whitechapel entitled 'Israel in London' illustrates the link between Jews, their food, their smell and, in this case, their poverty.

The district inhabited by the Israelitish colony in London cannot be said to be salubrious. At its best, from its situation, it has none too much fresh air; but the habits of denizens only make bad infinitely worse. To stroll down Middlesex Street on any ordinary day is to invite death from suffocation or poisoning. The fetid smells, the nauseous odours from dirty shops, fried-fish establishments, meat-shops, and unclean houses, are not easily to be described.[36]

Meanwhile, a fictional account, *Julie*, by Robert Blatchford, contains a description of east London 'Yiddish country', which characterizes the area as having:

> foul streets simmering in the heat, a blended and suffocating odour, as of fried onions and burnt bones, dirty clothing and stale fish, decaying vegetables and over-ripe fruit, unflushed sewers and kennels unswept, with whiffs from the gasworks and the tannery.[37]

Not all of those who made the link between Jews and fried fish did so in a negative way. An article entitled 'Among the Jews in London' simplistically declares that: 'The consumption of fried fish is the barometer of Hebrew happiness and prosperity.' The piece focuses upon the produce available in a shop owned by Mickey Joseph in Petticoat Lane:

> None but a Jew can appreciate it properly; none but a Jew can acquire the delicacy of taste in the matter of fried fish that is necessary to the eating of Mickey Joseph's middle pieces. To the profane Christian taste it is very good indeed. But it is a sight to see the fat, smooth-skinned Rachels and Leahs lift up their eyes in holy ecstasy as they take their first bite.[38]

By the end of the nineteenth century some writers had also made a link between fish eating and Jewish intelligence. This particular stereotype was summed up in the declaration that: 'Jews are especially brainy because of the great amount of fish they eat.'[39]

It seems clear that fried fish had a link with Jewish immigrants, in a both real and imagined sense, for most of the nineteenth century. While some writers, especially the Jewish Israel Zangwill, might have stressed this in a positive sense, the consumption and, more especially, the smell of fried fish, became another weapon with which anti-Semites could attack Jews. The link between Jews and fried fish faded away in the early twentieth century as fish and chips became associated with the working classes: the food and smell of the Jews became the food and smell of the poor. In both cases it had negative associations and would not change the negative image of fish and chips until it became the food of the ethnic majority in which class distinction (at least superficially) no longer mattered.

Foreign Purveyors of Fish and Chips

As well as eating fried fish, Jews also sold it during the nineteenth century, as some of the extracts quoted above indicate. In fact, they would continue to do so into the twentieth. *Kelly's Post Office London Directory* from 1923 lists 776 individuals who owned fried fish shops. A total of 148 of these have either obviously Jewish names, or at least Central European names. Those in the former category include eighteen Cohens, eleven Isaacs and eleven Levys. Although many of these remain concentrated in east London as a whole, rather than the inner East End (E1), some of them had premises in other parts of London. Eight of the eighteen Cohens lay in the core East End, together with others in Stratford, Great Western Road (W9) and Pentonville Road (N1). Those owned by individuals called Levy included properties in New Cross Road and Cartwright Gardens (WC1), while the name Isaac included only three properties in the East End heartland. Overall the 148 fish shops in London with Jewish-sounding names represented over 19 per cent of the total, while the list in *Kelly's* also contains a small number of shops owned by people with Italian names.[40] Jewish fish and chip shop owners included the father and uncles of Jessica Gould. Her grandparents, all from Russia, initially worked in the garment industry. While the shop of her father failed, those of her uncles succeeded 'cause they were in the right spots' in the West End. The locations of shops owned by her family included Commercial Road, Hammersmith and Soho.[41]

Jews would continue to play a role in the fish and chip trade into the post-war period, but by this time new ethnic groups had also entered the trade.[42] Other minorities, especially Italians, had owned fish and chip shops, especially in Wales and Scotland, from the early days of the establishment of the trade before the First World War and have continued to do so until the present. The majority of fish and chip shop owners since the end of the nineteenth century may well have consisted of members of the ethnic majority but both of the classic accounts of the fish and chip trade have recognized the importance of immigrants.

John Walton pointed out that our dish:

> expressed ethnic diversity as well as simplistic national solidarity, from the strong East End Jewish element in the early days of fish frying in London, through the strong Italian presence in the trade from the turn of the century, in urban Scotland and Ireland especially, to the growing importance of the Chinese and Greek Cypriots in the post-Second World War decades.[43]

Similarly Gerald Priestland asserted:

> There is an important ethnic aspect to Fish & Chips. Being at the bottom end of the social ladder, frying has constantly been passed down to the latest and lowliest arrivals upon the scene. In the late nineteenth century, in the East End of London, there were many continental Jews in the trade. Later, Italians took to it and there are colonies of English-speaking Italians in Newcastle, Glasgow, Edinburgh, Cardiff and Dublin to this day. The end of the Second World War brought in Cypriots, especially in London and Coventry. And more recently there have been invasions of Chinese and to a lesser extent Indo-Pakistani friers.[44]

Priestland offers an explanation for the presence of migrants in the fish and chip trade, but this remains partial. Before offering a full list of reasons, we can investigate the different ethnic groups which have played a role.

As the above extracts make clear, Italians spread our dish to Ireland, Wales and Scotland in particular. However, other groups also played a role. Pat O'Mara remembered that on the day when Britain declared war on Germany in 1914 he and his friends 'all hurried to John the Greek's fish and chip shop in St James Street' in Liverpool.[45] Whether John came from Cyprus, as numerous fish and chip shop owners would do by the 1960s, seems unclear.

Before 1945 Italians (along with Jews) predominated, especially in the Celtic fringes of Britain. In the case of Ireland it seems that Italian immigrants established the fish and chip trade and have continued to play a leading role until the present. The first fish and chip shops here emerged as the result of the efforts of migrants who came from six villages in the district of Casalattico in Latium not far from Rome, eventually making their way to Dublin via Paris, Scotland or various seaside resorts, where they would have observed the fish and chip trade.[46]

In Wales the role of Italians in the development of the spread of our dish needs contextualization against the background of their role as small businessmen, especially in the south of the country. An Italian survey from 1939 listed 302 Italian businesses in Wales, including 34 fish and chip shops. The major category consisted of cafés (187).[47] In the previous decade another account had stated that the 52 Italians in Merthyr Tydfil 'almost monopolize the fish and chip and ice-cream business'.[48] The classic account of the history of Italians in Wales suggests that the newcomers originated from the hill town of Bardi near Parma. They originally set themselves up as itinerant ice cream vendors but, during the winter, sold chips. Many of them eventually accumulated enough capital to become sedentary and sustained their businesses by importing further immigrants from Bardi.[49] This account implies a migrant entrepreneurial spirit and also suggests that people from the same region either copied or felt inspired by those similar to themselves, a pattern which would apply to other migrant groups working in the catering trade in twentieth-century Britain.

Most information on the years before 1945 survives on the Italians in Scotland, who came to play a key role in the fish and chip trade. By the 1930s 80 per cent of fish fryers in the country may have had Italian origins. Like their compatriots in Wales, they originated from distinct areas, meaning that a pattern of chain migration also evolved here. The earliest from the 1870s came from Barga, in the northern province of Lucca, and Picinisco 250 miles further south. Others followed from Emilia. Again mirroring the picture in Wales some of these newcomers, originally from rural backgrounds, set up either fish and chip shops or ice cream parlours throughout Scotland: in some cases, such as the business established by the father of Mary Contini in Cockenzie, they sold both.[50]

Two key themes, which would apply to many of the other immigrants who have become involved in the fish and chip trade, are evident in any analysis of Italian fryers in Scotland. The first of these consists of prejudice, often resulting in violence, especially of a drunken nature. This was exacerbated by the British government's decision to intern Italian males of military age following Mussolini's declaration of war on Britain in June 1940. Diana Corrieri, a teenage girl at the time, recalled seeing her father for the last time when the police arrived to arrest him 'in the chip shop frying fish and chips and they took him away in the dirty clothes he had on'.[51] Even when the war ended hostility survived amongst some Glasgow fish fryers, who opposed the return of Italians to the trade.[52]

The second theme is the narrative of hard work and ultimate reward (despite the experience of the Second World War), summed up in the phrase of Joe Pieri that:

> The history of the Italians in Scotland is a story of what can be achieved by people of lowly and underprivileged beginnings, with little or no education, and with nothing to rely on except their own inner strength and determination to survive and prosper, so as to provide for their families a future which they could not hope for in their land of birth.[53]

Similarly, Mary Contini recalled that even though her father 'made his livelihood frying fish and chips, he put every effort into making them the very best'; when filleting he 'worked with freezing cold water all the time'.[54] Pieri's outlook rests on his own experiences. His father had moved to Glasgow in 1924 and initially worked for another Italian fish and chip shop owner in Crown Street. When the proprietor wanted to return home for a year Francesco Pieri, Joe's father, took it over.[55] In 1931 Francesco purchased another Glasgow fish and chip business, the Savoy, which, according to his son, he transformed into one of the best in the city through dedication and hard work. Joe and his brother Ralph eventually took over the business when their father died in 1965.[56]

The story Joe Pieri tells involves the classic narrative of immigrant success, in this case through the medium of the fish and chip trade. While Italians continued to play a role in the trade after 1945, new groups became prominent. One of the most notable has consisted of the Greek Cypriots. Like the Italians, Greek Cypriots in the British fish and chip trade mostly came from rural backgrounds and became widely involved in the catering industry as a whole. By 1966 a total of 19.6 per cent of Cypriots in London worked for themselves at a time when the national figure for the whole of the population stood at 7.1 per cent.[57] While some of the newcomers would eventually open up recognizably Greek restaurants, especially from the 1970s, they also came to play a significant role in the fish and chip trade. As with many of the migrant movements into catering, ethnic employment clustering operated, by which individuals followed their countrymen already working in a particular sector. Greek Cypriots who worked in catering often did so shortly after arriving in Britain, suggesting a

An Italian fryer in Ayrshire during the 1920s.

high propensity for risk taking, but also reflecting a desire for self-sufficiency rooted in the fact that land- and home-ownership amongst the predominantly agrarian population in Cyprus had become the norm from as early as the sixteenth century, giving Cypriots 'a strongly developed ideology of property possession as both a right and a goal'. Those who moved to England did so for economic reasons, meaning a readiness to work long hours and to take risks.[58]

Kelly's Directories of London provide an indication of the role of Greek Cypriots and other migrant communities in the fish and chip trade. In 1954 we can identify sixteen Greek names amongst the fried fish shops listed, together with 23 Italian ones out of a total of around 800. At this stage Jews also continued to play a role. Nevertheless, because not all owners name their shops after themselves and do not always give them a name suggesting their place of origin, these figures are only the lowest possible estimate of migrant influence.[59] By 1975, when the number of London fried fish shops remained similar, at least 150 recognizably Greek Cypriot-owned businesses existed in the capital, although this again does not reflect the true picture. If we add to this those names of Turkish Cypriot, Chinese, Italian and other foreign origins, then it seems clear that migrants had come to play a major role in the fried fish trade by this time, a process which would continue as increasing diversification occurred in subsequent decades.[60]

The Eleftheriou family, which owns Grimsby Fisheries in Leicester, offers a good example of Greek Cypriot fish and chip shop owners. The father, Costas, moved to England in 1950, originally working in the West Midlands for Hovis and then in a Lyons restaurant in Granby Street, Birmingham. He subsequently worked for a Cypriot contact in Kingston upon Thames as a waiter before migrating to Coventry and buying a 'working man's restaurant'. He purchased his first fish and chip shop in Leicester from 'an Englishman' in 1966 and then bought Grimsby Fisheries. Costas's son Lefteris, who partly owns the shop, explained the different work ethics between the former English owner of Grimsby Fisheries and his own family:

The owner used to close to have a break between 6 and 7, you know . . . put the closed sign to have his break for an hour . . . He never used to open on Monday, he used to do Saturday. He used to close after lunch time . . . He was making enough you see.

In contrast, his parents had worked under 'hard conditions in Cyprus, like my father used to work on the land'. Although running a fish and chip shop in England 'was hard, it was much easier than the job they were doing there'.[61]

The Eleftheriou family offer just one of many examples of successful Greek Cypriot fish and chip shops, pointing to the fact that, like Italians, they often established family-based businesses in which brothers or several generations became involved. Costas Mbousia claimed that he had worked in the chip shop run by his parents in Manchester from the age of eleven and knew that he wanted to move into catering when leaving school, leading him to establish two 'traditional English fish and chip shops' in Manchester and its suburbs.[62] Similarly, Moisis Adamou purchased a business in 1962 and celebrated '50 years of continuous fish and chips service at Marlow Fish Bar in South London'.[63] One of the most famous Cypriot fryers, Mark Petrou, followed in his father's footsteps, together with his brother and eventually won the NFFF-sponsored National Fish and Chip Shop of the Year award in 2006. His father, Stavros, had initially opened a business in Shepherd's Bush in London in 1969, six years after settling in Britain, but then moved his family to Ramsey in Cambridgeshire to establish a business there. This reflects the pattern of the Greek Cypriot community, whose members, while heavily concentrated in London, have often left the capital to take over the running of fish and chip shops or other catering establishments elsewhere. The Petrou brothers eventually took over their father's business, now in Chatteris in Cambridgeshire, when he retired.[64] Michael Pili, who would become the first Cypriot president of the NFFF (a group whose hierarchy has remained overwhelmingly 'Anglo-Saxon') in 1998, was born in London in 1943 to Greek Cypriot parents who moved to Birmingham in the same year to open up a fish

Costas in Oadby, Leicester, originally established by a family of Greek
Cypriot origin and now owned by Sikhs, 2013.

and chip business. He entered the family business in 1960 and ran
shops in the Midlands until 1990, after which he became a consultant
to other fryers.[65]

Another migrant group which moved into the trade in significant
numbers after 1945 consists is that of the Chinese. Their patterns
resemble that of Cypriots and Italians in the sense that they have
become involved in catering generally and have tended to run
family businesses. The growth in the 'Chinese chippy' needs contextualization against the growth of Chinese migration to Britain in
the late 1950s and early 1960s. The newcomers mostly came to
Britain to work in the expansion of the Chinese restaurant trade,
which mushroomed from the second half of the 1950s. The 'Chinese
chippy', a particularly northern development, consisted of a former
fish and chip shop taken over by Chinese people which offered a
range of other products, including Chinese fast food. By 1984, 500
of these existed in the northwest alone; indeed, throughout Britain
there were as many as 7,000 Chinese restaurants by this time.[66]

Chinese chippy, Bristol, 1974.

Chinese fish and chip shops also existed in other parts of the country including the business owned by David Wong in Bristol, who, following the pattern elsewhere in the country, sold Chinese dishes as well as fish and chips. In this case the founder of the business, David's grandfather, originally ran it as a fish and chip shop when taking it over in 1946 and did not start selling Chinese food until the early 1970s in response to local demand.[67]

Evidence exists of racial hostility towards Chinese fryers, also experienced by other migrant groups. The Chinese had an association with the new takeaway culture, regarded as a major threat to the survival of the fish and chip trade since the 1960s. In 1976 the *Fish Trader* carried articles entitled 'Chinese are on the March' and 'Chinese Shop Poses Threat to Friers'.[68] The NFFF appear to have become aware of the hostility towards Chinese and other migrant groups from the 1960s and made efforts through the FFR asking its members to 'Be Patient with Immigrants'.[69] In 1989 the FFR also carried a series of letters allegedly written 'From a Chinese Chip Shop', giving the perspective of this particular ethnic group.[70]

Members of other minorities have also moved into the trade in recent decades, including South Asians, as evidenced by owners with names such as Zarar Gulbahar and Zohaib Hussain, as well as the development of halal fish and chips, cooked in oil rather than animal fat.[71] The most famous South Asian business is the fictional one which exists in the film *East is East* (dir. Damian O'Donnell, 1999), owned by Zahir 'George' Khan, a Pakistani immigrant married to a British Roman Catholic woman of Irish descent, whose multiracial children work with their parents in the family business in Salford. Interestingly, the French version of the film carried the title *Fish and Chips*. The themes it portrays, revolving around the issues of living between two cultures, provides a good metaphor for the ethnic complexity of our dish.

The Fish and Chip Shop as Melting Pot

In many ways the immigrants who moved to Britain to run fish and chip shops followed in the footsteps of British people from working-class backgrounds, especially in the early twentieth century, who viewed their shops as a type of business which required relatively little outlay but which could provide a means to a secure income and social mobility, especially through generations. The fish and chip shop has represented just one type of self-employment for migrants motivated not simply by the desire for profit but also by the difficulties of breaking into mainstream British occupations.[72] While most of the narratives cited above consist of success stories, some small-scale businessmen of migrant origins have experienced failure, especially those opening Indian restaurants.[73] Clearly, in view of the decline in the number of fish and chip shops since the 1950s some people in this trade must have experienced bankruptcy, including immigrants.

We can see fish and chip shops as a point of cross-cultural contact in which members of the ethnic majority (together with other ethnic groups) purchase a commodity which, as the twentieth century progressed, increasingly became a symbol of Britishness. We might see the fish and chip shop as a place which represents immigrant success and social mobility while the majority population remain trapped in their class roles, especially in early twentieth-century Scotland. At the same time they offer immigrants a way into mainstream British society, especially as, in many cases, their children and even grandchildren continue in the trade.

The origins of the dish also point to the fish and chip shop as a place of cross-cultural contact. While various theories exist for the emergence of fried potatoes, it seems indisputable that fish fried in batter became popular amongst Jews before becoming adopted by mainstream society. We can see fried fish as a symbol of Jewish integration moving, just as Jewish immigrants did, from the margins towards the centre of British society over the course of twentieth-century British history. The dish, while it has now become the ultimate symbol of Britishness, therefore has a whole series of associations with migrant groups.

FIVE

The Meanings of
Fish and Chips

Fish and chips emerged as a British meal during the course of the nineteenth century and by the second half of the twentieth had developed into *the* culinary symbol of national identity, having replaced even roast beef. Its move from the margins as the food of the Jews (in the case of fried fish) and then the poor occurred over a period of more than 100 years and the ethnic, national and social identity of the dish offers just one way of understanding it, to which we can add several others.

Food

In the first place we can place it within the food history of Britain. In this sense, it fits into wider developments in the changing consumption patterns, connected with the availability to the entire population of two new products: potatoes and fresh fish. The increasing popularity of the former came about as a result of increases in grain prices which took place in the first half of the nineteenth century, meaning that the use of potato as a staple began to become common not only in Ireland and northwest England – where poor soil made wheat cultivation problematic – but increasingly in the rest of the British Isles. To this we also need to add one of the most important developments resulting from industrialization, which in turn became the driver for further economic growth: the railways. Their arrival proved revolutionary, becoming a 'leading sector' in the words of one economic historian and further fuelling the growth of the coal and iron ore industries because of the demand it created for these products.[1] The other main benefit of the growth of the railways consisted of its ability to shrink the market. Products which had taken days to transport could now arrive in hours. Only in this way can we understand the spread of fried fish. It changed from a food which the majority of the British population had for centuries only eaten dried or preserved to one which they could now consume freshly fried. The early industrialization of Britain and its geographical nature as an island, with every part of the country within a few hours of a port once the railways took off, played a major role in the spread of fresh fried fish consumption in Britain compared with any other part of Europe.

John Walton has stressed how important fish and chips became as a staple food for the working classes by the early twentieth century. Although many middle-class commentators looked down on it, and continue to do so, it has always had nutritional benefits, despite the isolated cases of poisoning which happened in its early days and the health scares which have developed around fried food in recent decades. While suggesting that it increased working-class health *may* prove an exaggeration, it certainly improved their diets, providing vitamins, calories and protein in an age when most of the population found themselves engaged in manual labour. Walton stresses the fact that the middle classes simply ignored this improvement and instead focused on the fact that poor people ate this food, which reflected other aspects of their disorganized lives.[2]

Nevertheless, this stereotype does not simply come from the British middle classes, as it has also symbolized the poverty of the culinary heritage of the country. With the rise of pride in British cuisine in recent decades, partly as a reaction against new foods arriving from Europe and Asia, those who have written about British food usually feature fish and chips despite the fact that, however chefs may dress it up (even in the extreme manner of Heston Blumenthal) it remains a simple dish which requires just five ingredients: oil, potatoes, fish, flour and water. In any case, there seems little point in even going to the effort of cooking fish and chips at home, which involves using a large amount of oil, when a nearby takeaway can make a better version. In a global context fish and chips has come to symbolize the poverty of British cooking, especially when compared with the culinary heritage of Britain's nearest neighbour, France. In 2005 the French president, Jacques Chirac, asserted that only Finnish food was worse than British.[3] While the fish and chip trade, as well as British writers, may have tried to construct the dish in a positive manner as a symbol of Britishness, it has also become a symbol of the poverty of British cooking on a global scale.

The Takeaway

One of the stereotypes which has always circulated about fish and chips concerns the fact that it symbolizes the inability or unwillingness of British people – especially the working classes – to cook. Walton accepts that this easily available and ubiquitous food acted as a substitute for food cooked at home. It saved time for working-class families where both parents worked and also proved just as cheap as purchasing ingredients for cooking.[4]

Within the British context fish and chips becomes the first takeaway, which others have subsequently imitated. This does not mean to say that it became the first cooked food which British people purchased. Henry Mayhew pointed to the availability not just of fried fish on London's streets but also, for example, baked potatoes, sandwiches and hot peas. Nevertheless, these remained street foods. Fish-and-chip selling differs, and also begins a new trend, because its consumers purchase the product, by the beginning of the twentieth century, from a shop and, increasingly, by the 1920s and 1930s, from a restaurant. While street food has still not disappeared from Britain, the growth of the fish and chip shop and restaurant represents the sedentarization of street food so that Mayhew's purveyors become less common.

A variety of explanations present themselves for these developments including the evolution of stable working-class neighbourhoods based on terraced housing, which emerged in the later Victorian and Edwardian periods in urban locations throughout Britain. They differed from the recently arrived and often transitory populations which had characterized the beginnings of industrialization in the early nineteenth century, outlined by commentators such as Mayhew in London and Frederick Engels in Manchester.[5] While late Victorian and Edwardian Britons still lived in relative poverty, their lives had become more stable in terms of residence due to the rise of terraced housing.[6] This stability offered the background to the emergence and proliferation of fish and chip shops based in a particular locality in the decades before and after the First World War as it meant the traders could rely on a stable clientele. As people who lived in urban areas could purchase cooked food on their doorstep, they did not need to prepare their evening meal.

This trend has continued until the present: Joanna Blythman pointed out that in 2003 'Britain ate more ready meals than the rest of Europe put together.'[7] Britons don't even have to bother to go to the effort of turning on the oven or microwave involved in 'cooking' a ready meal because of the ubiquity of the takeaway. A reading of Blythman actually resembles some of the commentators in the early twentieth century, quoted by Walton, who complained about the inability of the working classes to cook. This offers one explanation for the development of fish and chips at the end of the nineteenth century.

The rapidity of industrialization also played a role as it meant that Britons, unlike, for example, French people, lost contact with the land from which they originated and did not develop the concept of *terroir*, focusing upon the local origins of specific foods.[8] Despite the construction of the idea of fish and chips as a national food after 1945, Walton's research clearly points to the fact that it had actually become so in reality by the 1920s. Why would Britons need to worry about the source of their food, when they could purchase a cheap, nutritious and delicious meal already cooked for them by somebody else? Why should they therefore devote time to cooking?

Fish and chips sets in motion trends in British food consumption which continue into the second half of the twentieth century, including the lack of concern for the origins of food or even its constituent parts. We need to understand the fish and chip shop as the first takeaway, a sedentary producer of cheap, cooked food, which would witness new developments from the 1950s. The main reason for the hostility which some fryers displayed towards Chinese takeaways lay precisely in the fact that they copied the patterns which the fryers had originally established of offering cheap, cooked food to the same customer base. Chinese and Indian takeaways as well as Cypriot- and Turkish-owned kebab shops, which often combine with fish and chip selling, imitate the patterns established at the end of the nineteenth century by the fish and chip trade. All of these outlets offer cheap, cooked food. Those who purchase it may have some concern about taste, but not about the origins of the food they eat. Both the takeaway and the restaurants which evolve from them, whether fish and chip, Chinese or Indian, remain informal places to dine, contrasting with upmarket restaurants, which many working-class people find stuffy and too expensive.

Fish and chips, like its successors, has also offered a business opportunity for those who wished to enter the trade. As Walton first emphasized, and as many of the stories quoted above stress, purchasing a shop allowed many people with limited capital to experience financial security and social mobility. While those who owned these shops worked long hours in many cases – from the purchase and preparation of the fish and potatoes in the morning to the selling and cleaning up in the evening – they have required a limited financial outlay.

Fish and chip businesses have remained small in scale with few employees, largely because they remain family concerns in which wives and children play a central role. In numerous cases fathers pass their businesses down to their children in a process which can last several generations. This began in the early twentieth century but continues today. As well as offering ambitious working- or lower middle-class people with a small amount of capital opportunities, the fish and chip shop has also allowed immigrants, whether Jewish, Italian, Cypriot or Chinese, a chance at business success without needing to have any great culinary skills, although successful fryers would have to keep their clientele satisfied by offering good-quality food in the light of competition from other fish and chip shops before 1945, and other takeaways since the 1950s. Again, fish and chips provides the template followed subsequently by other takeaway owners selling food chosen along overtly ethnic lines, in the sense that the owners of Chinese and Indian takeaways open up their businesses mainly for financial reasons rather than because they have any great culinary skills. While many such restaurants may employ chefs and waiters from outside the immediate family, they remain small in scale and also produce dishes using the cheapest possible ingredients, whether frozen vegetables or factory-farmed meat.

Despite the fact that many fish and chip shop owners and their families have experienced social mobility, it seems clear that others, like their Chinese and Indian successors, have faced bankruptcy in view of the decline in the number of fish and chip businesses in Britain over the past 50 years. In many ways the survival of the independent fish and chip shop, as well as the independent takeaway more generally, represents one of the most remarkable aspects in the history of fish and chips in Britain. Despite the increasing dominance of large companies as employers in Britain, which, in the catering trade, has included several hamburger, fried chicken, fish and chip and pizza chains, fish and chip shops have survived as largely independent concerns, as have Chinese and Indian takeaways and the kebab shop. Explanations for this might include the durability of taste passed from one generation to another as well as the fact that fish and chips represents good-quality, real food sold at a cheap price. At the same time, from the 1920s, fish and chip shops have increasingly diversified from peas through to pies, chicken and kebabs. Multinationals also tend to operate on a large scale which has meant that they have not penetrated every row of shops in every locality in Britain whether in a big city or small town, therefore leaving a space for the independent takeaway. However, the survival of the fish and chip shop and the takeaway more generally also suggests the continued existence of an entrepreneurial spirit in Britain amongst immigrants and natives alike. Perhaps nothing better symbolizes the survival of small business in Britain, over more than a century, than the fish and chip shop.

Britishness

While fish and chips remains rooted in Britain, we need to disentangle the reality and marketing of its Britishness. In terms of reality, it seems indisputable that, whatever its origins, since the end of the nineteenth century it has remained British in the sense that those who have consumed it have tended to do so within Britain, especially amongst working-class communities. Some globalization has taken place as the presence of fish and chip shops in the Mediterranean, former British colonies and the USA would indicate. However, each of these has a British element. In the Mediterranean fish and chips offers a taste of home either for long-term British residents or holidaymakers. At the same time, emigrants from Britain have often opened up many of the fish and chip shops which have appeared in Canada, South Africa and Australia.

Once we move to the USA the myth of Britishness comes into play. As we have seen, since the end of the Second World War all foods have developed an ethnic identity as a result of globalization, increasing international migration and marketing. The designation of our dish along ethnic lines partly occurred through the effort of food writers, the fish and chip trade and the press in Britain. However, the process also occurs on an international scale. Fish and chips could only find a space in the ethnicized American food market, constructed by waves of immigration, if it had its own identity.[9] As the extracts from the *New York Times* quoted above have stressed, this has taken place in a simplistic way, in which the caricatured Briton eats fish and chips. Once the Harry Ramsden franchise went global, it used the same stereotypes. The marriage of fish and chips may have taken place in Victorian London and developed within Britain during the course of a century with no consciousness of its identity, but once it encountered foreign foods which moved into Britain and then went global, those who marketed it felt that they had to stress its Britishness in order to ensure its survival.

Immigration

Fish and chips offers a symbol of the impact, importance and changing nature of immigration to Britain over the past two centuries. The evidence for the origin of chips as a foreign product remains inconclusive and it seems possible that frying potatoes might have evolved at a similar time in several European locations, including France, Britain and Belgium. Some sort of cultural transfer as a result of migration may have occurred but evidence has not emerged to prove this.

On the other hand, fried battered fish had Jewish origins, as Victorian sources indicate. While anti-Semites viewed its consumption and the consequences of this negatively in the form of smell, Jewish writers, whether of cookbooks or literary works, wrote about it positively, as seen most clearly in Israel Zangwill's *Children of the Ghetto*. Zangwill viewed it as a Jewish national dish at a high point in the diasporic history of this community, over half a century before the establishment of Israel.[10] At some stage in the early Victorian period a process of cultural transfer must have taken place when the gentile majority started to consume the food of the Jews.[11] The arrival of the railways and fresh fish would have played a key role in this process, as few gentiles (especially amongst the poor) are likely to have eaten the cold fried fish described by Hannah Glasse. The new method of transportation meant that the entire population could eat hot, fried fresh fish. The earliest references to fish frying in batter in London involve Jews but during the course of the 1840s and 1850s Gentiles also began to fry and consume it as evidenced by the descriptions provided by Henry Mayhew. While the availability of fresh fish played a major role in this cultural transfer, so did taste, as several descriptions of Jewish fish frying during the Victorian period indicate.

Jews therefore played a significant role in the genesis of fried battered fish consumption in Britain during the nineteenth century. We can consequently view fish and chips as an immigrant food by origin provided by one of the most significant ethnic groups in the country until the second half of the twentieth century. The spread of the dish also has close connections to new waves of immigrants to the extent that the ownership of fish and chip shops reflects the immigration history of Britain. While members of the ethnic majority have owned most of the businesses which have existed in Britain, new waves of immigrants have always moved into the trade. Thus Italian ownership reflects the arrival of this group into the country in the decades leading up to the First World War, while the entry into the trade by Greek Cypriots and the Chinese points to the arrival of these two groups after 1945.[12]

Finally an acceptance of the Jewish origins of fish and chips also points to the establishment of a pattern which would take off from the 1950s. In the same way as fried fish moved from a Jewish product to one adopted by the ethnic majority, so did the process of cultural transfer facilitate the adaptation of Chinese food and curry in Britain from the 1940s onwards. Part of the process of acceptance involved changing to suit to British tastes. The Chinese food sold in Britain differs from that eaten in China, while curry essentially represents the food of the colonial British in India, which came home at the end of Empire with returning Anglo-Indians and newly arrived immigrants.[13] Fried fish sets this sequence of events in motion and also indicates that while it may have represented an anti-Semitic stereotype, it also offers a way to break down these stereotypes as it changes from the food of the Jews to the food of the poor to eventually the food of the British.

References

Abbreviations

BL   British Library
FFR   *Fish Friers Review*
FTG   *Fish Trades Gazette*
NFFF   National Federation of Fish Friers

1 Origins

1 FFR, June 1965; FFR, November 1968; *The Times*, 27 September 1968; Gerald Priestland, *Frying Tonight: The Saga of Fish and Chips* (London, 1972), pp. 66–7; *Guardian*, 10 November 1965; *Daily Mail*, 9 May 2010.

2 Mark Petrou, *Fish and Chips: A National Treasure: Celebrating 150 Years of Britain's Favourite Dish* (Chatteris, 2010), p. 25.

3 *Daily Express*, 7 January 2010.

4 *Daily Mail*, 9 May 2010.

5 Pierre Picton and Rod Harrod, *A Gourmet's Guide to Fish and Chips* (Stroud, 1990), pp. xii–iv (this title was originally published in London, 1966 with Picton as sole author); Petrou, *Fish and Chips*, p. 25.

6 Chatchip, *The Fish Frier and His Trade* (London, 1924). The description of Loftas comes from John K. Walton, *Fish & Chips and the British Working Class, 1870–1940* (Leicester, 1992), p. 5.

7 FTG, 12 March 1921. Mayhew is discussed below.

8 Charles Latham Cutting, *Fish Saving: A History of Fish Processing from Ancient to Modern Times* (London, 1955), pp. 14–24.

9 Brian M. Fagan, *Fish on Friday: Fasting, Feasting and the Discovery of the New World* (New York, 2006), pp. 3–23; Priestland, *Frying Tonight*, pp. 25–8.

10 C. Anne Wilson, *Food and Drink in Britain* (London, 1973), pp. 16–20.

11 Ibid., pp. 20–25; Richard Tames, *Feeding London: A Taste of History* (London, 2003), p. 11.

12 Wilson, *Food and Drink*, pp. 25–30; Fagan, *Fish on Friday*, pp. 27–57; Cutting, *Fish Saving*, pp. 25–52; Moira Buxton, 'Fish Eating in Medieval England', in *Fish: Food from the Waters*, ed. Harlan Walker (Totnes, 1998), pp. 51–7; Colin Spencer, *British Food: An Extraordinary Thousand Years of History* (London, 2002), pp. 54–5.

13 Mark Kurlansky, *Cod: A Biography of the Fish that Changed the World* (London, 1998); Fagan, *Fish on Friday*, pp. 219–89; W. Jeffrey Bolster, *The Mortal Sea: Fishing the Atlantic in the Age of Sail* (London, 2012), pp. 40–49.

14 Priestland, *Frying Tonight*, pp. 27–8; Fagan, *Fish on Friday*, pp. 14–23.

15 Kurlansky, *Cod*, p. 24.

16 Cutting, *Fish Saving*, p. 32; Fagan, *Fish on Friday*, pp. 241–4.

17 Wilson, *Food and Drink*, pp. 46–9.

18 Cutting, *Fish Saving*, pp. 214–15.

19 Ibid., pp. 203–7.

20 W. H. Chaloner, 'Trends in Fish Consumption', in *Our Changing Fare: Two Hundred Years of British Food Habits*, ed. T. C. Barker, J. C. McKenzie and John Yudkin (London, 1966), pp. 97–102.

21 Robert May, *The Accomplisht Cook* (London, 1671), pp. 301, 328–9, 334–7, 342–3, 371.

22 *The Compleat Cook or the Whole Art of Cookery* (London, 1694), pp. 50–61, 66–7, 72–5.

23 T. Hall, *The Queen's Royal Cookery* (London, 1709), p. 122.

24 Charles Carter, *The Complete Practical Cook* (London, 1730), pp. 69–70.

25 Hannah Glasse, *The Art of Cookery Made Plain and Easy* (Edinburgh, 1781), p. 433.

26 M. Radcliffe, *A Modern System of Domestic Cookery* (Manchester, 1823), p. 150.

27 Charles Latham Cutting, 'Fish Preservation as a Factor in the
    Extension of Supply', in *Fish in Britain*, ed. T. C. Barker and John
    Yudkin (London, 1971), p. 25.

28 Cutting, *Fish Saving*, p. 217.

29 Fish Association, *The Second Report of the Committee of the Fish
    Association for the Benefit of the Community Respecting the Measures
    to be Adopted for the Supply of the Metropolis and its Neighbourhood*
    (London, 1813).

30 George Dodd, *The Food of London* (London, 1856), p. 344;
    Chaloner, 'Trends', pp. 106–7.

31 Dodd, *Food of London*, pp. 351, 352.

32 Henry Mayhew, *London Labour and the London Poor* [1861], vol. 1
    (London, 1968), p. 69.

33 Chaloner, 'Trends', pp. 107–9.

34 Ibid., p. 105; Cutting, 'Fish Preservation', p. 26; FTG, 8 November
    1919.

35 Cutting, *Fish Saving*, pp. 217–20, 231–6, 249–58.

36 Redcliffe N. Salaman, *The History and Social Influence of the Potato*
    (Cambridge, 1949), pp. 1–145; Larry Zuckerman, *The Potato: From
    the Andes in the Sixteenth Century to Fish and Chips* (London, 1989),
    pp. 3–10; Archibald Findlay, *The Potato: Its History and Culture
    with Descriptive List of Varieties Raised* (Cupar-Fife, 1905), p. 1.

37 Findlay, *The Potato*, p. 2; Thomas P. McIntosh, *The Potato: Its
    History, Varieties, Cultures and Diseases* (London, 1927), pp. 6–10;
    T.E.H.W. Krichauff, 'The Tercentenary of the Introduction of the
    Potatoes into England', *Journal of the Royal Horticultural Society*,
    XIX (1895–6), pp. 224–5.

38 Zuckerman, *Potato*, pp. 17, 31–2.

39 Ibid., pp. 47–60; Salaman, *History and Social Influence of the Potato*,
    pp. 424–50.

40 Salaman, *History and Social Influence of the Potato*, p. 454.

41 Ibid., pp. 456–542; Zuckerman, *Potato*, pp. 57–67, 98–120,
    128–58; Spencer, *British Food*, pp. 225–9.

42 May, *Accomplisht Cook*, p. 273.

43 Wilson, *Food and Drink*, pp. 218–19.

44 Nick Groom, 'William Henry Ireland: From Forgery to Fish and
    Chips', in *Cultures of Taste/Theories of Appetite: Eating Romanticism*,
    ed. Timothy Morton (London, 2004), pp. 29–30, 32.

45 Radcliffe, *Modern System*, p. 360.

46 French fried potatoes are considered in chapter Three.

47 Charles Dickens, *Oliver Twist* [1838] (Oxford, 1999), p. 196.

48 Charles Dickens, *A Tale of Two Cities* [1859] (Oxford, 1998), p. 33.

49 Ibid., p. 374. I owe this reference to Professor Robert Canton of De Montfort University.

50 Mayhew, *London Labour and the London Poor*, vol. I, p. 62.

51 Ibid., pp. 160–5.

52 Ibid., pp. 165–70.

53 Ibid., pp. 172–5.

54 See chapter Three.

55 *Morning Chronicle*, 4 October 1837; *London Standard*, 4 October 1837; *Bell's Life in London and Sporting Chronicle*, 8 October 1937.

56 *Era*, 31 May 1840.

57 *Odd Fellow*, 7 November 1840.

58 *Leicester Mercury*, 13 August 1842; *Liverpool Mercury*, 12 August 1842.

59 *Morning Post*, 27 June 1851.

60 Watts Phillips, *The Wild Tribes of London* (London, 1855), pp. 66–7.

61 Walton, *Fish & Chips*, p. 25.

62 Petrou, *Fish and Chips*, pp. 27–31.

63 Priestland, *Frying Tonight*, pp. 64–7. Malin's shop in Old Ford Road faced demolition in 1972, for which see FFR, August 1972.

64 Alexis Soyer, *A Shilling Cookery Book for the People* (London, 1860), p. 114; *Jewish Manual: Or Practical Information in Jewish and Modern Cookery with a Collection of Valuable Recipes and Hints Relating to the Toilette* [London, 1846] (New York, 1983), p. 92.

65 Ibid., pp. 114–15.

66 *Girl's Own Paper*, 6 May 1882.

67 Soyer, *Shilling Cookery*, p. 28.

68 Piscator, *Practical Treatise on the Choice and Cookery of Fish* (London, 1854), pp. 173–4.

69 Mrs John B. Thwaites, *Fish Cookery* (Liverpool, 1883), pp. 11, 15–16.

70 James Greenwood, *Unsentimental Journeys: Or Byways of the Modern Babylon* (London, 1867), p. 13.

71 *Morning Post*, 24 February 1865.

72 *Morning Post*, 26 November 1872.

73 'Cheap Shops in London', *Chambers's Journal*, 15 March 1879.
74 Metropolitan Board of Works, *Report of the Chief Officer of the Metropolitan Fire Brigade, on the state of the Brigade, and the Fires in London during the Year 1867* (London, 1868), pp. 3, 14; Metropolitan Board of Works, *Report of the Chief Officer of the Metropolitan Fire Brigade, on the state of the Brigade, and the Fires in London during the Year 1888* (London, 1889), pp. 3, 12.
75 *Manchester Courier*, 27 November 1866.
76 *Leicester Journal*, 2 July 1869; *Leicester Chronicle*, 3 July 1869.
77 *Morning Post*, 26 November 1872.
78 *Newcastle Courant*, 23 October 1868.
79 *Leicester Chronicle and Leicester Mercury*, 12 October 1878.
80 *Daily News*, 12 April 1884.
81 *The Times*, 19 March 1875; *Standard*, 1 April 1875.
82 'Fish Diet', *All Year Round*, 16 June 1883, p. 18.
83 Walton, *Fish & Chips*, pp. 5, 26–30.
84 Ibid., pp. 6–7.
85 D. J. Oddy, 'Working Class Diets in Late Nineteenth Century Britain', *Economic History Review*, XXIII (1970), p. 322.
86 *Young Folks Paper*, 14 November 1885.
87 Panikos Panayi, *Spicing Up Britain: The Multicultural History of British Food* (London, 2008), pp. 162–76.
88 FTG, 2 September 1905.
89 Walton, *Fish & Chips*, p. 27.
90 Priestland, *Frying Tonight*, pp. 73–4.
91 FTG, 27 March 1920. The business issues connected with fish and chip shops receive detailed attention in Walton, *Fish & Chips*, pp. 52–71.
92 Elizabeth Buettner, 'Chicken Tikka Masala, Flock Wallpaper, and "Real" Home Cooking: Assessing Britain's "Indian" Restaurant Traditions', *Food and History*, VII (2009), pp. 203–29.
93 Chaloner, 'Trends', p. 110.
94 Chatchip, *Fish Frier*, pp. 13–22.
95 Priestland, *Frying Tonight*, pp. 89–96, 122.
96 Chatchip, *Fish Frier*, pp. 200–9; Walton, *Fish & Chips*, pp. 111–17.
97 Walton, *Fish & Chips*, p. 8; Priestland, *Frying Tonight*, pp. 72–3; N. Moser, *From Sea to Table* (London, 1911), pp. 17–23.

2 Evolution

1 *FTG*, 2 April 1921.
2 Ministry of Agriculture, Fisheries and Food, *Report on the Marketing of Potatoes in England and Wales* (London, 1926), p. 59.
3 *Manchester Guardian*, 15 January 1931.
4 Sea-fish Commission for the United Kingdom, *Second Report: The White Fish Industry* (London, 1936), p. 52.
5 Ministry of Food, *The Urban Working-class Household Diet 1940 to 1949: First Report of the National Food Survey Committee* (London, 1951), pp. 27–8; *FTG*, 12 May and 29 December 1945.
6 *FFR*, October 1954; R. A. Taylor, *The Economics of White Fish Distribution in Great Britain* (London, 1960), pp. 141–2.
7 White Fish Authority, *Fifth Annual Report and Accounts for the Year ended 31 March 1956* (London, 1956), p. 41.
8 *FFR*, October 1955.
9 *FTG*, 22 December 1956.
10 *The Times*, 7 September 1957.
11 *Third Special Report from the Select Committee on Agriculture with Report from the Sub-Committee on Fisheries* (London, 1968), p. 89.
12 *FFR*, June 1964.
13 *Daily Mirror*, 6 July 1968.
14 Peter Ford, 'Excessive Competition in the Retail Trades: Changes in the Number of Shops, 1901–1931', *Economic Journal*, XLV (1935), pp. 501–8.
15 *FTG*, 2 April 1921; White Fish Authority, *Fifth Annual Report*, p. 41.
16 Chatchip, *The Fish Frier and His Trade* (London, 1924).
17 H. T. Reeves, *The Modern Fish-frier*, 2 vols (London, 1933).
18 Greville Havenhand, *Nation of Shopkeepers* (London, 1970), p. 173.
19 Joe Pieri, *River of Memory: Memoirs of a Scots-Italian* (Edinburgh, 2006), pp. 20–22.
20 Havenhand, *Nation of Shopkeepers*, pp. 173, 174.
21 John K. Walton, *Fish & Chips and the British Working Class, 1870–1940* (Leicester, 1992), p. 69.
22 *FTG*, 7 May 1927.
23 Ibid., 4 June 1927.
24 Ibid., 14 May 1927; *Fish Traders' Weekly*, 14 December 1937.

25 Ibid., 1 March 1938. For another example of such praise see, for example, Jack Bedford, *Frying Times: Reflections and Observations of Life by a Bradford Fish Frier* (Ilfracombe, 1993), p. 27.

26 Havenhand, *Nation of Shopkeepers*, p. 173.

27 FFR, January 1958.

28 White Fish Authority, *Fifth Annual Report*, p. 42.

29 Chatchip, *Fish Frier*, pp. 31–7, 49–56.

30 FTG, 17, 24 January 1914.

31 Ibid., 23 January 1932.

32 Ibid., 27 January 1951.

33 Walton, *Fish & Chips*, p. 34.

34 Reeves, *Modern Fish-frier*, pp. 79–97.

35 FTG, 13 February 1932.

36 Ibid., 18 January 1936.

37 Ibid., 22 August 1936.

38 BL, Mass Observation Online, File Report 685, 'Holidays', May 1941, p. 17.

39 FFR, January 1958.

40 Ibid., November 1964.

41 Taylor, *Economics of White Fish Distribution*, p. 142.

42 FTG, 19 February 1927.

43 Ibid., 14 November 1936.

44 Ibid., 6 August 1966, 8 June 1968.

45 Ibid., 27 February 1932, 18 January 1936, 13 January 1951; Gerald Priestland, *Frying Tonight: The Saga of Fish and Chips* (London, 1972), p. 84.

46 Priestland, *Frying Tonight*, pp. 79–87; Walton, *Fish & Chips*, pp. 111–36; Roy Shipperbottom, 'Fish and Chips', in *Fish: Food from the Waters*, ed. Harlan Walker (Totnes, 1998), p. 266; FTG, 10, 17, 24 December 1921; FFR, January 1968, October 1969.

47 FTG, 28 May, 4, 18, 25 June 1921.

48 Ibid., 6 April, 30 July 1921.

49 Ibid., 2 July, 29 October 1921.

50 Priestland, *Frying Tonight*, pp. 89–99; Walton, *Fish & Chips*, pp. 47–50.

51 Walton, *Fish & Chips*, p. 101; Shipperbottom, 'Fish and Chips', p. 272; Priestland, *Frying Tonight*, pp. 105–6.

52 FTG, 10 September 1921.

53 Reeves, *Modern Fish-frier*, pp. 136–64.

54 Priestland, *Frying Tonight*, p. 106.

55 FTG, 1 October 1921.

56 Reeves, *Modern Fish-frier*, pp. 351–67.

57 Ibid., pp. 201–8; Chatchip, *Fish Frier*, pp. 128–38.

58 *The Times*, 7 September 1957.

59 *Manchester Guardian*, 15 January 1931.

60 Chatchip, *Fish Frier*, pp. 163–6.

61 Henry Mayhew, *London Labour and the London Poor* [1861], vol. 1 (London, 1968), pp. 161–3.

62 Chatchip, *Fish Frier*, pp. 166–7.

63 FTG, 17 July 1920.

64 *Frier*, 3 September 1921.

65 *Guardian*, 10 February 1959.

66 FTG, 19 August 1961.

67 FFR, January 1957.

68 Ibid., December 1956; *The Times*, 7 September 1957.

69 BL, Mass Observation Online, 'The Pub and the People: A Worktown Study By Mass Observation', London, 1943, p. 119.

70 BL, Mass Observation Online, File Report 685, 'Holidays', May 1941, p. 18.

71 Ministry of Food, *Fish Cookery* (London, 1948), p. 111.

72 Good Housekeeping Institute, *Mac Fisheries Fish Cookery* (London, 1955), p. 12.

73 See, for example, Elizabeth Lucas, *A Pretty Kettle of Fish* (London, 1935); James Beard, *James Beard's Fish Cookery* (London, 1955).

74 It is important to note that these figures are estimates. Other sources suggest a significantly higher number of fish-and-chip shops during the 1970s and 1980s.

75 A. G. Williams, 'Fish and Chips and the Fast Food Revolution', *Fish Industry Review*, 1 (1977), pp. 7–9; *The Times*, 24 September 1971; *Fish Trader*, 29 March 1980.

76 *Guardian*, 23 June 1971.

77 FTG, 14 June 1975.

78 *Guardian*, 26 January 1976.

79 Acumen Marketing Group, *A Report on the Take Away Food Market in Britain* (London, 1978), pp. 4, 10–11, 26, 115.

80 Euromonitor, *The Hotel and Catering Industry* (London, 1982), p. 29.

81 Sea Fish Industry Authority Fishery Economics Research Unit, *British Survey of Eating Out – Fish: July 1981–June 1982* (Edinburgh, 1983), p. 6.

82 David Lennon, 'Fish and Chips Revolution', *Europe* (October 1992), pp. 40–41.

83 MINTEL, *Eating Out 1992* (London, 1992), pp. 1–3, 40, 52–6.

84 *Observer*, 19 January 2003; *The Times*, 9 February 2009.

85 MINTEL, 'Eating Out Review – UK – July 2012', http://academic.mintel.com, accessed 2 October 2012.

86 Panikos Panayi, *Spicing Up Britain: The Multicultural History of British Food* (London, 2008), pp. 162–3.

87 Acumen Marketing Group, *Report on Take Away Food Market*, pp. 78–9, 92.

88 FFR, March 1970.

89 *Fish Trader*, 30 November 1985.

90 FTG, 29 March 1975.

91 *Fish Trader*, 23 October 1976, 22 November 1980, 27 April, 11, 25 May 1985.

92 MINTEL, *Eating Out 1992*, p. 42.

93 FFR, May 1952, February, March 2003; *Guardian*, 25 April 1972, 5 December 1980, 26 June 1998; *Financial Times*, 14 November 1996; Charles Derwent, 'Wild About Harry's', *Management Today*, January 1991, p. 68; 'About Harry's', www.harryramsdens.co.uk, accessed 2 October 2012.

94 John Burnett, *England Eats Out: A Social History of Eating Out in England from 1830 to the Present* (London, 2004), p. 313.

95 Panayi, *Spicing*, pp. 171, 173.

96 FFR, 12 June 1971.

97 *Fish Trader*, 28 April 1990.

98 FFR, June 2003.

99 Ibid., February 1999.

100 Ibid., September 2004.

101 Ibid., March 2005.

102 Ibid., March 1994.

103 Ibid., September 1994.

104 Ibid., August 1970.

105 Ibid., May 2012.

106 Ibid, June 2004.

107 Pierre Picton and Road Harrod, *A Gourmet's Guide to Fish and Chips* (Stroud, 1990); this title was originally published in London in 1966 with Picton as sole author.

108 *The Times*, 13 August 2011.

109 *FTG*, 19 April 1975.

110 *Fish Trader*, 13 July 1985.

111 Acumen Marketing Group, *Report on Take Away Food Market*, p. 114.

112 Mark Petrou, *Fish and Chips: A National Treasure: Celebrating 150 Years of Britain's Favourite Dish* (Chatteris, 2010), p. 43; *The Times*, 22 March 2010, 9 December 2011.

113 Petrou, *Fish and Chips*, pp. 40–43.

114 *Fast Food and Fish and Chips*, October 2004.

115 Carol Parsons, *Introduction to Fish Frier Practice* (London, 1988), pp. 72–5. See also the feature on McCain's chips in the *FTG*, 8 May 1971.

116 Ibid; *FFR*, June 1989.

117 *Guardian*, 31 July 2012; 'Harry's At Home', www.harryramsdens.co.uk, accessed 2 October 2012.

118 *Great British Menu* (London, 2006); James Martin, *Great British Dinners* (London, 2003).

119 *Mirror*, 4 June 1997.

120 See chapter Three.

3 Britishness

1 John K. Walton, *Fish & Chips and the British Working Class, 1870–1940* (Leicester, 1992), p. 137.

2 Charles Dickens, *Oliver Twist* [1838] (Oxford, 1999), p. 196.

3 Reprinted in *Trewman's Exeter Flying Post*, 20 March 1856.

4 Charles Dickens, *A Tale of Two Cities* [1859] (Oxford, 1998), p. 33.

5 Henry Mayhew, *London Labour and the London Poor*, vol. 1 [1861] (London, 1968), p. 168.

6 George Gissing, *Workers in the Dawn* [1880] (Brighton, 2010), p. 7.

7 H. D. Lowry, 'Unknown London 1: The Mysteries of Walworth Road', *Windsor Magazine* (January 1895), pp. 30–36.

8 *FTG*, 2 September 1905.

9   *Morning Post*, 26 November 1872.
10 George Orwell, *The Road to Wigan Pier* [1937] in *Orwell's England* (London, 2001), pp. 116, 382.
11 Robert Roberts, *The Classic Slum* (London, 1971), p. 107.
12 *North-eastern Daily Gazette*, 7 April 1897.
13 Sarah Elizabeth Francis, 'Author's Note', *Ladybird Lane* (London, 1962).
14 Francis, *Ladybird Lane*, pp. 103–4.
15 *Northern Echo*, 11 December 1891.
16 *The Times*, 2 March 2004.
17 Tim Lobstein, *Fast Food Facts* (London, 1988); *Observer*, 25 January 2000.
18 Ben Rogers, *Beef and Liberty: Roast Beef, John Bull and the English Nation* (London, 2003).
19 Panikos Panayi, *Spicing Up Britain: The Multicultural History of British Food* (London, 2008), pp. 12–37.
20 *New York Times*, 14 October 1928.
21 *Hull Daily Mail*, 20 December 1929.
22 *Manchester Guardian*, 16 January 1931.
23 Philip Harben, *Traditional Dishes of Britain* (London, 1953), p. 7.
24 Ibid., p. 115.
25 Ibid., p. 116.
26 Adrian Bailey, *The Cooking of the British Isles* (London, 1970), pp. 111–15.
27 *Observer*, 1 March 1992; *The Times*, 1 March 1992; *Guardian*, 29 February 1992.
28 Mark Petrou, *Fish and Chips: A National Treasure: Celebrating 150 Years of Britain's Favourite Dish* (Chatteris, 2010).
29 James Martin, *Great British Dinners* (London, 2003), p. 87; Gary Rhodes, *New British Classics* (London, 1999), pp. 169–70.
30 *Great British Menu* (London, 2006), p. 83.
31 Heston Blumenthal, *In Search of Total Perfection* (London, 2009), pp. 253–67.
32 *New York Times*, 4 April 1960.
33 Ibid., 26 February 1958.
34 Ibid., 18 April 1962.
35 Ibid., 9 March 1993.
36 Ibid., 25 July 1989.
37 Ibid., 28 February 1979.

38 *Guardian*, 22 November 2003.
39 *Daily Mirror*, 7 January 2010; *Daily Express*, 7 January 2010.
40 *The Times*, 28 April 2004.
41 'Best of Britain: Fish 'n' Chips Tops "Best of British" Poll',
    www.ihgplc.com, 25 June 2008.
42 FFR, May 1952.
43 Ibid., September 1968.
44 Ibid., June 1976.
45 Ibid., July 2007.
46 FTG, 21 April 1956.
47 *Fried Fish Caterer*, 31 January 1980.
48 FFR, March 1992.
49 Ibid., December 1963.
50 Ibid., September 1998.
51 Ibid., July 2009.
52 Walton, *Fish & Chips*, p. 40.
53 Ibid., p. 38; Shane Hegarty, *The Irish (& Other Foreigners): From
    the First People to the Poles* (Dublin, 2009), pp. 161–4.
54 *Fish Traders' Weekly*, 26 April 1938. See also: *Fish Traders' Weekly*,
    7 July 1938; FTG, 4 April 1936.
55 Gerald Priestland, *Frying Tonight: The Saga of Fish and Chips*
    (London, 1972), p. 113.
56 Ibid., pp. 113–14; Walton, *Fish & Chips*, p. 39; FFR, 30 April 1980,
    June 2010; *Fried Fish Caterer*, 30 April 1980; FTG, 30 April 1932;
    www.chumleywarners.com.au, accessed 26 October 2012;
    'Reviews', 'Chumley Warner's Traditional British Fish and Chips',
    http://expatdirectory.telegraph.co.uk, accessed 26 October 2012.
57 Priestland, *Frying Tonight*, p. 113.
58 FTG, 30 April 1932; Hilda Gerber, *Fish Fare for South Africans*
    (Port Elizabeth, 1945), pp. 23–6.
59 *Frier*, 1 August, 1 October 1923.
60 Priestland, *Frying Tonight*, p. 111; FFR, May 1952; Ole Sparenberg,
    'How the Germans did not Approriate Fish and Chips: The Case
    of the Fischbratküche in the 1920s and 1930s', in *Travelling Goods,
    Travelling Moods: Varieties of Cultural Appropriation (1850–1950)*,
    ed. Christian Huck and Stefan Bauernschmidt (Frankfurt, 1950),
    pp. 61–78.
61 See www.nordsee.com/at/produkte/190/fish-und-chips, accessed
    23 November 2012.

62 FFR, August, September 1993.

63 *The Times*, 31 July 1999, 4 March 2000, 9 September 2010.

64 FFR, August 1998.

65 *New York Times*, 22 December 2004.

66 FFR, April 1960.

67 *New York Times*, 12 November 1899.

68 FTG, 27 September, 18 October 1919, 5 September 1936; *Fish Traders' Weekly*, 25 August 1936.

69 FFR, January, September 1969, May 1977; *Observer*, 5 November 1978; FTG, 21 August 1971; Priestland, *Frying Tonight*, pp. 114–19.

70 *Worcester Telegram and Gazette*, 30 August 1993, 6 February 2008; *The Times*, 24 August 2001; *Economist*, 7 June 2001.

71 Hasia R. Diner, *Hungering for America: Italian, Irish and Jewish Foodways in the Age of Migration* (London, 2001); Linda Keller Brown and Kay Mussell, eds, *Ethnic and Regional Foodways in the United States: The Performance of Group Identity* (Knoxville, TN, 1985); Donna R. Gabaccia, *We Are What We Eat: Ethnic Food and the Making of Americans* (London, 1998).

72 *Guardian*, 20 July 1993; *Irish Times*, 15 July 1995; *The Times*, 12 December 1998.

73 Donna R. Gabaccia, 'Pizza, Pasta and Red Sauce: Italian or American', *History in Focus* 11: Migration, www.history.ac.uk, accessed 1 November 2012; Lizzie Collingham, *Curry: A Biography* (London, 2005); Kenneth Lo, *Chinese Food* (London, 1972).

74 FFR, January 1968.

75 *Northern Echo*, 28 August 2001.

76 *The Times*, 7 August 2004.

77 *Observer*, 9 May 1976.

78 FTG, 21 December 1946; Roy Bainton, *The Long Patrol: The British in Germany* (Edinburgh, 2003), pp. 203–5; Navy, Army and Air Force Institutes, www.naafi.co.uk, accessed 27 December 2012.

79 Karen O'Reilly, *The British on the Costa del Sol* (London, 2000), pp. 89–93.

80 *Punch*, 28 July 1971.

81 FFR, July 1995, October 1996, September 1997.

82 This information was gathered when I actually stopped to eat a pork chop here on 3 September 2007.

4 Ethnicity

1 'Top UK Dish 'Hooked French First', http://news.bbc.co.uk, accessed 19 December 2012.

2 'Know Your Enemy', www.stormfront.org/forum/showthread. php?t=90992&page=5&pp=10, accessed 19 December 2012.

3 *The Times*, 20 February, 20 May 2010.

4 *Daily Mail*, 9 May 2010.

5 Clarissa Dickson Wright, *A History of English Food* (London, 2011), Kindle location 6013.

6 Claudia Roden, *The Book of Jewish Food: An Odyssey from Samarkand to New York* (New York, 1996), p. 113.

7 *Jewish Chronicle*, 15 December 2006.

8 Roden, *Book of Jewish Food*, p. 114.

9 *Glasgow Herald*, 14 April 1868.

10 Israel Zangwill, *Children of the Ghetto* [1893] (Chestnut Hill, MA, 2006), pp. 48–9.

11 Alexis Soyer, *A Shilling Cookery Book for the People* (London, 1860), p. 28.

12 Eliza Acton, *Modern Cookery for Private Families* (London, 1865), p. 607.

13 *The Jewish Manual: Or Practical Information in Jewish and Modern Cookery with a Collection of Valuable Recipes and Hints Relating to the Toilette* [London, 1846] (New York, 1983), p. 38.

14 Florence Greenberg, *Jewish Cookery Book*, 9th edn (London, 1988), p. 50.

15 See chapter One.

16 Charles Dickens, *A Tale of Two Cities* [1859] (Oxford, 1998), p. 33.

17 Karen Hess, 'The Origins of French Fries', *Petits Propos Culinaires*, LXVIII (2001), pp. 39–48; Maryann Tebben, '"French" Fries: France's Culinary Identity from Brillat-Savarin to Barthes', *Convivium Artum* (Spring 2006), p. 3. For Soyer see, for example: Ruth Brandon, *The People's Chef: Alexis Soyer, A Life in Seven Courses* (Chichester, 2005); and Ruth Cowen, *Relish: The Extraordinary Life of Alexis Soyer, Victorian Celebrity Chef* (London, 2006).

18 Peter Scholliers, *Food Culture in Belgium* (London, 2009), pp. 131–3.

19 Tebben, '"French" Fries', pp. 2–7.

20 See also above pp. 33–4.

21 Panikos Panayi, *Immigration, Ethnicity and Racism in Britain, 1815–1945* (Manchester, 1994), pp. 50–51. But see the recently published Debra Kelly and Martyn Cormick, eds, *A History of the French in London: Liberty, Equality, Opportunity* (London, 2013), which does not engage with the issues discussed here despite containing an essay entitled 'Experiencing French Cookery in Nineteenth-century London' by Valerie Mars.

22 Colin Holmes, *Anti-Semitism in British Society, 1876–1939* (London, 1979); Polly Pinsker, 'English Opinion and Jewish Emancipation (1830–1860)', *Jewish Social Studies*, XIV (1952), pp. 51–94.

23 Robert D. Butterworth, 'The Significance of Fagin's Jewishness', *Dickensian*, CV (2009), pp. 213–24; Harry Stone, 'Dickens and the Jews', *Victorian Studies*, II (1959), pp. 223–53; Todd M. Endelman, *The Jews of Britain, 1656–2000* (London, 2002), pp. 79–126.

24 *Morning Chronicle*, 7 April 1824.

25 *Morning Post*, 22 September 1853.

26 Anne and Roger Cowen, *Victorian Jews through British Eyes* (Oxford, 1986).

27 *Age and Argus*, 28 September 1844.

28 *Chambers's Edinburgh Journal*, 2 December 1848.

29 *City Press*, 12 June 1858.

30 Watts Phillips, *The Wild Tribes of London* (London, 1855), pp. 67–8.

31 *Morning Post*, 11 September 1849.

32 'Down Whitechapel Way', *Household Words*, 1 November 1851.

33 George Augustus Sala, 'Imaginary London', *Belgravia* (December 1872), p. 202.

34 Holmes, *Anti-Semitism*.

35 Bernard Gainer, *The Alien Invasion: The Origins of the Aliens Act of 1905* (London, 1972); Lloyd P. Gartner, *The Jewish Immigrant in England, 1870–1914* (London, 1960).

36 George A. Wade, 'Israel in London: How the Hebrew Lives in Whitechapel', *English Illustrated Magazine* (August 1900), pp. 405–6.

37 Robert Blatchford, *Julie: A Study of a Girl* (London, 1900), p. 33.

38 *Freeman's Journal and Commercial Advertiser*, 4 April 1893.

39 See John M. Shaftesley, 'Culinary Aspects of Anglo-Jewry', in *Studies in the Cultural Life of the Jews in England*, ed. Issachar Ben-Ami and Dov Noy (Jerusalem, 1975), p. 389.

40 *The Post Office London Directory with County Suburbs for 1923* (London, 1923), pp. 2410–11.

41 Interview with Jessica Gould, 13 April 2004.

42 *Post Office London Directory for 1954* (London, 1954), pp. 2252–3.

43 John K. Walton, *Fish & Chips and the British Working Class, 1870–1940* (Leicester, 1992), p. 2.

44 Gerald Priestland, *Frying Tonight: The Saga of Fish and Chips* (London, 1972), p. 20.

45 Pat O'Mara, *The Autobiography of a Liverpool Irish Slummy* (London, 1934), p. 139.

46 Walton, *Fish & Chips*, p. 38; Shane Hegarty, *The Irish (& Other Foreigners): From the First People to the Poles* (Dublin, 2009), pp. 162–3; *Irish Times*, 12 September 1998.

47 See Colin Hughes, *Lime, Lemon and Sarsaparilla: The Italian Community in Wales, 1881–1945* (Bridgend, 1991), pp. 47–8.

48 J. Ronald Williams, 'The Influence of Foreign Nationalities on the Life of the People of Merthyr Tydfil', *Sociological Review*, XVIII (1926), p. 152.

49 Hughes, *Lime*.

50 Walton, *Fish & Chips*, pp. 37–8; Wendy Ugolini, *Experiencing the War as the 'Enemy Other': Italian Scottish Experience in World War II* (Manchester, 2011), pp. 28–30; Mary Contini, *Dear Francesca: An Italian Journey of Recipes Recounted with Love* (London, 2003), p. 241; Joe Pieri, *The Scots-Italians: Recollections of an Immigrant* (Edinburgh, 2005), p. 14.

51 Ugolini, *Experiencing the War*, pp. 30–31, 121.

52 FTG, 31 March, 21 April 1945.

53 Pieri, *The Scots-Italians*, p. 15.

54 Contini, *Dear Francesca*, p. 242.

55 Joe Pieri, *River of Memory: Memoirs of a Scots-Italian* (Edinburgh, 2006), pp. 5–7.

56 Joe Pieri, *Tales of the Savoy: Stories from a Glasgow Café* (Glasgow, 1999).

57 Panikos Panayi, *An Ethnic History of Europe Since 1945: Nations, States and Minorities* (London, 2000), p. 65.

58 Floya Anthias, *Ethnicity, Class, Gender and Migration: Greek Cypriots in Britain* (Aldershot, 1992), p. 58.

59 *Post Office London Directory for 1954*, pp. 2252–3.

60 *Kelly's Post Office London Directory* (London, 1975), pp. 1837–9, 1889–92.

61 Interview of Lefteris and Costas Elefheriou, 5 April 2004.

62 FFR, July 2007.

63 *Parikiaki*, 5 April 2012.

64 Mark Petrou, *Fish and Chips: A National Treasure: Celebrating 150 years of Britain's Favourite Dish* (Chattcris, 2010), pp. 45–62; Kathy Burrell, *Moving Lives: Narratives of Nation and Migration among Europeans in Post-war Britain* (Aldershot, 2006), pp. 10, 149, 161.

65 FFR, June, August 1998.

66 Anthony Shang, *The Chinese in Britain* (London, 1984), pp. 25–6; J.A.G. Roberts, *China to Chinatown: Chinese Food in the West* (London, 2002), pp. 172–6; Susan Chui Chie Baxter, 'A Political Economy of the Ethnic Chinese Catering Industry' PhD Thesis, Aston University, 1988.

67 FFR, December 1974.

68 *Fish Trader*, 29 May, 10 July 1976.

69 FFR, June 1969.

70 Ibid., March, April, October 1989.

71 Ibid., July 2003, March 2012, May 2012.

72 Sarah Hackett, 'From Rags to Restaurants: Self-determination, Entrepreneurship and Integration amongst Muslim Immigrants in Newcastle upon Tyne in Comparative Perspective, 1960s–1990s', *Twentieth Century British History*, XXIV (2013).

73 Trevor Jones and Monder Ram, 'South Asian Businesses in Retreat? The Case of the UK', *Journal of Ethnic and Migration Studies*, XXIX (2003).

5 The Meanings of Fish and Chips

1 The concept of leading sector in industrialization is used by W. W. Rostow, *The Process of Economic Growth*, 2nd edn (Oxford, 1960), pp. 261–73, although he provides different examples.

2 John K. Walton, *Fish & Chips and the British Working Class, 1870–1940* (Leicester, 1992), pp. 137–67.

3 *Independent*, 6 July 2005.

4 Walton, *Fish and Chips*, pp. 137–61.
5 Friedrich Engels, *The Condition of the Working Class in England* [1845] (London, 1987), especially pp. 68–110.
6 Richard Rodgers, *Housing in Urban Britain, 1780–1914* (Cambridge, 1995).
7 Joanna Blythman, *Bad Food Britain: How a Nation Ruined Its Appetite* (London, 2006), pp. xv–xvi.
8 Julia Abramson, *Food Culture in France* (London, 2007), pp. 33–7.
9 As an introduction see Donna R. Gabaccia, *We Are What We Eat: Ethnic Food and the Making of Americans* (London, 1998).
10 See, for example, David Vital, *A People Apart: The Jews in Europe, 1789–1939* (Oxford, 1999).
11 See Stefan Manz and Panikos Panayi, 'Refugees and Cultural Transfer to Britain: An Introduction', in *Refugees and Cultural Transfers to Britain*, ed. Stefan Manz and Panikos Panayi (Abingdon, 2013), pp. 11–21.
12 Panikos Panayi, *An Immigration History of Britain: Multicultural Racism since 1800* (London, 2010), pp. 37–45.
13 Kenneth Lo, *Chinese Food* (London, 1972); Lizzie Collingham, *Curry: A Biography* (London, 2005).

Bibliography

Archival Material and Official Publications

British Library, Mass Observation Online, File Report 685: 'Holidays' (May 1941)

British Library, Mass Observation Online, 'The Pub and the People: A Worktown Study By Mass Observation' (London, 1943)

Metropolitan Board of Works, *Report of the Chief Officer of the Metropolitan Fire Brigade, on the state of the Brigade, and the Fires in London during the Year 1867* (London, 1868)

——, *Report of the Chief Officer of the Metropolitan Fire Brigade, on the state of the Brigade, and the Fires in London during the Year 1888* (London, 1889)

Ministry of Agriculture, Fisheries and Food, *Report on the Marketing of Potatoes in England and Wales* (London, 1926)

Ministry of Food, *Fish Cookery* (London, 1948)

——, *The Urban Working-class Household Diet 1940 to 1949: First Report of the National Food Survey Committee* (London, 1951)

Post Office Directories of London (Kelly's), 1913, 1923, 1954, 1975, 1984

Sea-fish Commission for the United Kingdom, *Second Report: The White Fish Industry* (London, 1936)

Sea Fish Industry Authority Fishery Economics Research Unit, *British Survey of Eating Out – Fish: July 1981–June 1982* (Edinburgh, 1983)

Third Special Report from the Select Committee on Agriculture with Report from the Sub-committee on Fisheries (London, 1968)

White Fish Authority, *Fifth Annual Report and Accounts for the Year ended 31 March 1956* (London, 1956)

Newspapers and Periodicals

Age and Argus
Bell's Life in London and Sporting
    Chronicle
Chambers's Edinburgh Journal
City Press
Daily Express
Daily Mail
Daily Mirror
Daily News
Economist
Era
Financial Times
Fish Friers Review
Fish Trader
Fish Traders' Weekly
Fish Trades Gazette
Freeman's Journal and Commercial
    Advertiser
Fried Fish Caterer
Frier
Girl's Own Paper
Glasgow Herald
Guardian
Hull Daily Mail
Independent

Irish Times
Jewish Chronicle
Leicester Chronicle
Leicester Chronicle and Leicester
    Mercury
Leicester Journal
Leicester Mercury
Liverpool Mercury
London Standard
Manchester Courier
Manchester Guardian
Morning Chronicle
Morning Post
Newcastle Courant
New York Times
North-eastern Daily Gazette
Northern Echo
Observer
Odd Fellow
Parikiaki
Punch
The Times
Trewman's Exeter Flying Post
Worcester Telegram and Gazette
Young Folks Paper

Other Published Material

Abramson, Julia, *Food Culture in France* (London, 2007)
Acton, Eliza, *Modern Cookery for Private Families* (London, 1865)
Acumen Marketing Group, *A Report on the Take Away Food Market in Britain* (London, 1978)
Anthias, Floya, *Ethnicity, Class, Gender and Migration: Greek Cypriots in Britain* (Aldershot, 1992)
Bailey, Adrian, *The Cooking of the British Isles* (London, 1970)
Bainton, Roy, *The Long Patrol: The British in Germany* (Edinburgh, 2003)
Barker, T. C., J. C. McKenzie and John Yudkin, eds, *Our Changing*

Fare: Two Hundred Years of British Food Habits (London, 1966)

Baxter, Susan Chui Chie, 'A Political Economy of the Ethnic Chinese Catering Industry', PhD Thesis, Aston University, 1988

Beard, James, *James Beard's Fish Cookery* (London, 1955)

Bedford, Jack, *Frying Times: Reflections and Observations of Life by a Bradford Fish Frier* (Ilfracombe, 1993)

Blatchford, Robert, *Julie: A Study of a Girl* (London, 1900)

Blumenthal, Heston, *In Search of Total Perfection* (London, 2009)

Blythman, Joanna, *Bad Food Britain: How a Nation Ruined Its Appetite* (London, 2006)

Bolster, W. Jeffrey, *The Mortal Sea: Fishing the Atlantic in the Age of Sail* (London, 2012)

Brandon, Ruth, *The People's Chef: Alexis Soyer, A Life in Seven Courses* (Chichester, 2005)

Brown, Linda Keller, and Kay Mussell, eds, *Ethnic and Regional Foodways in the United States: The Performance of Group Identity* (Knoxville, TN, 1985)

Buettner, Elizabeth, 'Chicken Tikka Masala, Flock Wallpaper, and "Real" Home Cooking: Assessing Britain's "Indian" Restaurant Traditions', *Food and History*, VII (2009) pp. 203–9

Burnett, John, *England Eats Out: A Social History of Eating Out in England from 1830 to the Present* (London, 2004)

Burrell, Kathy, *Moving Lives: Narratives of Nation and Migration among Europeans in Post-war Britain* (Aldershot, 2006)

Butterworth, Robert D., 'The Significance of Fagin's Jewishness', *Dickensian*, CV (2009), pp. 213–24

Buxton, Moira, 'Fish Eating in Medieval England', in *Fish: Food from the Waters*, ed. Harlan Walker (Totnes, 1998), pp. 51–7

Carter, Charles, *The Complete Practical Cook* (London, 1730)

Chaloner, W. H., 'Trends in Fish Consumption', in *Our Changing Fare: Two Hundred Years of British Food Habits*, ed. T. C. Barker, J. C. McKenzie and John Yudkin (London, 1966), pp. 94–114

Chatchip, *The Fish Frier and His Trade* (London, 1924)

Collingham, Lizzie, *Curry: A Biography* (London, 2005)

The Compleat Cook or the Whole Art of Cookery (London, 1694)

Contini, Mary, *Dear Francesca: An Italian Journey of Recipes Recounted with Love* (London, 2003)

Cowen, Anne, and Roger Cowen, *Victorian Jews through British Eyes* (Oxford, 1986)

Cowen, Ruth, *Relish: The Extraordinary Life of Alexis Soyer, Victorian Celebrity Chef* (London, 2006)

Cutting, Charles Latham, 'Fish Preservation as a Factor in the Extension of Supply', in *Fish in Britain*, ed. T. C. Barker and John Yudkin (London, 1971)

——, *Fish Saving: A History of Fish Processing from Ancient to Modern Times* (London, 1955)

Derwent, Charles, 'Wild About Harry's', *Management Today* (January 1991)

Dickens, Charles, *Oliver Twist* [1838] (Oxford, 1999)

——, *A Tale of Two Cities* [1859] (Oxford, 1998)

Diner, Hasia R., *Hungering for America: Italian, Irish and Jewish Foodways in the Age of Migration* (London, 2001)

Dodd, George, *The Food of London* (London, 1856)

'Down Whitechapel Way', *Household Words*, 1 November 1851, pp. 126–31

Endelman, Todd M., *The Jews of Britain, 1656–2000* (London, 2002)

Engels, Friedrich, *The Condition of the Working Class in England* [1845] (London, 1987)

Euromonitor, *The Hotel and Catering Industry* (London, 1982)

Fagan, Brian M., *Fish on Friday: Fasting, Feasting and the Discovery of the New World* (New York, 2006)

Findlay, Archibald, *The Potato: Its History and Culture with Descriptive List of Varieties Raised* (Cupar-Fife, 1905)

Fish Association, *The Second Report of the Committee of the Fish Association for the Benefit of the Community Respecting the Measures to be Adopted for the Supply of the Metropolis and its Neighbourhood* (London, 1813)

'Fish Diet', *All Year Round* (16 June 1883), pp. 16–19

Ford, Peter, 'Excessive Competition in the Retail Trades: Changes in the Number of Shops, 1901–1931', *Economic Journal*, XLV (1935), pp. 501–8

Francis, Sarah Elizabeth, *Ladybird Lane* (London, 1962)

Gabaccia, Donna R., *We Are What We Eat: Ethnic Food and the Making of Americans* (London, 1998)

——, 'Pizza, Pasta and Red Sauce: Italian or American', *History in Focus* 11: Migration, www.history.ac.uk, accessed 1 November 2012

Gainer, Bernard, *The Alien Invasion: The Origins of the Aliens Act of 1905* (London, 1972)

Gartner, Lloyd P., *The Jewish Immigrant in England, 1870–1914* (London, 1960)

Gerber, Hilda, *Fish Fare for South Africans* (Port Elizabeth, 1945)

Gissing, George, *Workers in the Dawn* [1880] (Brighton, 2010)

Glasse, Hannah, *The Art of Cookery Made Plain and Easy* (Edinburgh, 1781)

Good Housekeeping Institute, *Mac Fisheries Fish Cookery* (London, 1955)

Great British Menu (London, 2006)

Greenberg, Florence, *Jewish Cookery Book*, 9th edn (London, 1988)

Greenwood, James, *Unsentimental Journeys: Or Byways of the Modern Babylon* (London, 1867)

Groom, Nick, 'William Henry Ireland: From Forgery to Fish and Chips', in Timothy Morton, ed., *Cultures of Taste/Theories of Appetite: Eating Romanticism* (London, 2004), pp. 21–40

Hackett, Sarah, 'From Rags to Restaurants: Self-determination, Entrepreneurship and Integration amongst Muslim Immigrants in Newcastle upon Tyne in Comparative Perspective, 1960s–1990s', *Twentieth Century British History*, XXIV (2013), pp. 132–54

Hall, T., *The Queen's Royal Cookery* (London, 1709)

Harben, Philip, *Traditional Dishes of Britain* (London, 1953)

Havenhand, Greville, *Nation of Shopkeepers* (London, 1970)

Hegarty, Shane, *The Irish (& Other Foreigners): From the First People to the Poles* (Dublin, 2009)

Hess, Karen, 'The Origins of French Fries', *Petits Propos Culinaires*, LXVIII (2001), pp. 39–48

Holmes, Colin, *Anti-Semitism in British Society, 1876–1939* (London, 1979)

Hughes, Colin, *Lime, Lemon and Sarsaparilla: The Italian Community in Wales, 1881–1945* (Bridgend, 1991)

Jewish Manual: Or Practical Information in Jewish and Modern Cookery with a Collection of Valuable Recipes and Hints Relating to the Toilette [London, 1846] (New York, 1983)

Jones, Trevor, and Monder Ram, 'South Asian Businesses in Retreat? The Case of the UK', *Journal of Ethnic and Migration Studies*, XXIX (2003), pp. 485–500

Kelly, Debra, and Martyn Cormick, eds, *A History of the French in London: Liberty, Equality, Opportunity* (London, 2013)

Krichauff, T.E.H.W., 'The Tercentenary of the Introduction of the Potato into England', *Journal of the Royal Horticultural Society*, XIX (1895–6), pp. 224–7

Kurlansky, Mark, *Cod: A Biography of the Fish that Changed the World* (London, 1998)

Lennon, David, 'Fish and Chips Revolution', *Europe*, October 1992

Lo, Kenneth, *Chinese Food* (London, 1972)

Lobstein, Tim, *Fast Food Facts* (London, 1988)

Lowry, H. D., 'Unknown London I: The Mysteries of Walworth Road', *Windsor Magazine* (January 1895), pp. 129–36

Lucas, Elizabeth, *A Pretty Kettle of Fish* (London, 1935)

McIntosh, Thomas P., *The Potato: Its History, Varieties, Cultures and Diseases* (London, 1927)

Martin, James, *Great British Dinners* (London, 2003)

May, Robert, *The Accomplisht Cook* (London, 1671)

Mayhew, Henry, *London Labour and the London Poor*, vol. I [1861] (London, 1968)

Manz, Stefan, and Panikos Panayi, eds, *Refugees and Cultural Transfers to Britain* (Abingdon, 2013)

MINTEL, *Eating Out 1992* (London, 1992)

Moser, N., *From Sea to Table* (London, 1911)

Oddy, D. J., 'Working-class Diets in Late Nineteenth-century Britain', *Economic History Review*, XXIII (1970), pp. 314–23

O'Mara, Pat, *The Autobiography of a Liverpool Irish Slummy* (London, 1934)

O'Reilly, Karen, *The British on the Costa del Sol* (London, 2000)

Orwell, George, *The Road to Wigan Pier* [1937] in *Orwell's England* (London, 2001)

Panayi, Panikos, *An Ethnic History of Europe Since 1945: Nations, States and Minorities* (London, 2000)

——, *Immigration, Ethnicity and Racism in Britain, 1815–1945* (Manchester, 1994)

——, *An Immigration History of Britain: Multicultural Racism since 1800* (London, 2010)

——, *Spicing Up Britain: The Multicultural History of British Food* (London, 2008)

Parsons, Carol, *Introduction to Fish Frier Practice* (London, 1988)

Petrou, Mark, *Fish and Chips: A National Treasure: Celebrating 150 years of Britain's Favourite Dish* (Chatteris, 2010)

Phillips, Watts, *The Wild Tribes of London* (London, 1855)

Picton, Pierre, and Rod Harrod, *A Gourmet's Guide to Fish and Chips* (Stroud, 1990)

Pieri, Joe, *River of Memory: Memoirs of a Scots-Italian* (Edinburgh, 2006)
——, *The Scots-Italians: Recollections of an Immigrant* (Edinburgh, 2005)
——, *Tales of the Savoy: Stories from a Glasgow Café* (Glasgow, 1999)
Pinsker, Polly, 'English Opinion and Jewish Emancipation
    (1830–1860)', *Jewish Social Studies*, XIV (1952), pp. 51–94
Piscator, *Practical Treatise on the Choice and Cookery of Fish* (London,
    1854)
Priestland, Gerald, *Frying Tonight: The Saga of Fish and Chips* (London,
    1972)
Radcliffe, M., *A Modern System of Domestic Cookery* (Manchester, 1823)
Reeves, H. T., *The Modern Fish-frier*, 2 vols (London, 1933)
Rhodes, Gary, *New British Classics* (London, 1999)
Roberts, J.A.G., *China to Chinatown: Chinese Food in the West* (London,
    2002)
Roberts, Robert, *The Classic Slum* (London, 1971)
Roden, Claudia, *The Book of Jewish Food: An Odyssey from Samarkand to
    New York* (New York, 1996)
Rodgers, Richard, *Housing in Urban Britain, 1780–1914* (Cambridge,
    1995)
Rogers, Ben, *Beef and Liberty: Roast Beef, John Bull and the English Nation*
    (London, 2003)
Rostow, W. W., *The Process of Economic Growth*, 2nd edn (Oxford, 1960)
Sala, George Augustus, 'Imaginary London', *Belgravia* (December 1872),
    pp. 199–208
Salaman, Redcliffe N., *The History and Social Influence of the Potato*
    (Cambridge, 1949)
Scholliers, Peter, *Food Culture in Belgium* (London, 2009)
Shaftesley, John M., 'Culinary Aspects of Anglo-Jewry', in Issachar Ben-
    Ami and Dov Noy, eds, *Studies in the Cultural Life of the Jews in
    England* (Jerusalem, 1975), pp. 367–99
Shang, Anthony, *The Chinese in Britain* (London, 1984)
Shipperbottom, Roy, 'Fish and Chips', in *Fish: Food from the Waters*,
    ed. Harlan Walker (Totnes, 1998), pp. 264–73
Soyer, Alexis, *A Shilling Cookery Book for the People* (London, 1860)
Sparenberg, Ole, 'How the Germans did not Approriate Fish and Chips:
    The Case of the Fischbratküche in the 1920s and 1930s', in
    *Travelling Goods, Travelling Moods: Varieties of Cultural
    Appropriation (1850–1950)*, ed. Christian Huck and Stefan
    Bauernschmidt (Frankfurt, 1950), pp. 61–78

Spencer, Colin, *British Food: An Extraordinary Thousand Years of History* (London, 2002)

Stone, Harry, 'Dickens and the Jews', *Victorian Studies*, II (1959), pp. 223–53

Tames, Richard, *Feeding London: A Taste of History* (London, 2003)

Taylor, R. A., *The Economics of White Fish Distribution in Great Britain* (London, 1960)

Tebben, Maryann, '"French" Fries: France's Culinary Identity from Brillat-Savarin to Barthes', *Convivium Artum* (Spring 2006)

Thwaites, Mrs John B., *Fish Cookery* (Liverpool, 1883)

Ugolini, Wendy, *Experiencing the War as the 'Enemy Other': Italian Scottish Experience in World War II* (Manchester, 2011)

Vital, David, *A People Apart: The Jews in Europe, 1789–1939* (Oxford, 1999)

Wade, George A., 'Israel in London: How the Hebrew Lives in Whitechapel', *English Illustrated Magazine* (August 1900), pp. 404–10

Walker, Harlan, ed., *Fish: Food from the Waters* (Totnes, 1998)

Walton, John K., *Fish & Chips and the British Working Class, 1870–1940* (Leicester, 1992)

Williams, A. G., 'Fish and Chips and the Fast Food Revolution', *Fish Industry Review*, I (1977), pp. 7–9

Williams, J. Ronald, 'The Influence of Foreign Nationalities on the Life of the People of Merthyr Tydfil', *Sociological Review*, XVIII (1926), pp. 145–52

Wilson, C. Anne, *Food and Drink in Britain* (London, 1973)

Wright, Clarissa Dickson, *A History of English Food* (Kindle Edition, 2011)

Zangwill, Israel, *Children of the Ghetto* [1893] (Chestnut Hill, MA, 2006)

Zuckerman, Larry, *The Potato: From the Andes in the Sixteenth Century to Fish and Chips* (London, 1989)

Interviews carried out by Panikos Panayi

Elefheriou, Lefteris and Costas, 5 April 2004
Gould, Jessica, 13 April 2004

Acknowledgements

I would like to thank the history research committee of De Montfort University and the Scouloudi Foundation for providing funding, which financed visits to the British Library at St Pancras and Colindale and to the National Federation of Fish Friers in Leeds. I would also like to acknowledge the assistance of Professors Tony Kushner, Peter Atkins and Peter Scholliers. Finally the staff of the National Federation of Fish Friers, especially Denise Dodd, the general secretary, and Joe Varley ensured that my visit in March 2013 proved enjoyable, productive, interesting and tasty (especially as I visited on the day of a training course for fryers).

Photo Acknowledgements

The author and the publishers wish to express their thanks to the below sources of illustrative material and /or permission to reproduce it.

Len and Doreen Dee: p. 98; The National Federation of Fish Friers (NFFF): pp. 14, 71, 93, 95, 130; Karen O'Reilly: p. 103; Panikos Panayi: pp. 8, 42, 56, 67, 73, 75, 83, 86, 99, 102, 105, 119, 129; Rex Features: p. 91; Mark Sandle: p. 92; Derek Ward: p. 23; Victorian Web: pp. 82, 117 (images scanned by Jacqueline Banerjee).

Index